Norman chancel at Hanslope

THE OLD PARISH CHURCHES
OF BUCKINGHAMSHIRE
Mike Salter

FOLLY PUBLICATIONS

ACKNOWLEDGEMENTS

The photographs in this book were taken by the author and the plans are largely based on his field surveys between 1973 and 2008. A few brass rubbings and old photographs in the author's collections have also been used. Many thanks are due to Ian Rennie of Nuneaton, Anne Ling of Denham and Jean Cuddeford formerly of Bedford for help with fieldtrips and acquiring information on Buckinghamshire churches, and also to Paul and Allan at Aspect Design for help with the cover artwork.

ABOUT THIS BOOK

As with the other books in this series (see full list on the inside of the back cover) this book concentrates on the period before the Industrial Revolution of the late 18th century. Most furnishings and monuments after 1800 are not mentioned, but additions and alterations to the fabric usually are, although in less detail. Churches founded after 1800 to serve new suburban areas (see page 11) do not appear in the gazetteer or on the map. Each former village church now lying within Milton Keynes has its own entry in the gazetteer, the entry for Milton Keynes referring to the village of that name only.

The book is inevitably very much a catalogue of dates and names, etc. It is intended as a field guide and for reference rather than to be read straight from cover to cover. Occasionally there is a comment about the setting of a church but on the whole not much is said about their locations or atmosphere. In a few cases notable features of a building may lie outside the scope of this book. Visit them and judge for yourself. The book is intended to be used in conjunction with the O.S. 1:50,000 scale Landranger maps and a two letter and six figure grid reference appears after each place-name and dedication. Numbers of the maps required are: 152, 153, 164, 165, 166, 175 & 176.

Plans redrawn from originals in the author's notebooks are reproduced to a common scale of 1:400, which is a standard scale used for almost all the churches in the other titles in this series and allows some useful comparisons. The buildings were measured in metres and only metric scales are given. Three metres almost equals ten feet for those still wanting imperial measures. A hatching system common to all the plans is used to denote the different periods of work. Note that some things are difficult on convey on small scale plans (eg stones of one period being reset or reused in a later period). In some cases walling is shown on a plan as being of a specific century when it is in fact difficult to date with accuracy. There are for instance several towers that may be either late 14th or early 15th century, or were begun on one period and completed in another, whilst there is uncertainty as to how much of the outer walling of certain narrow late 12th and early 13th century aisles has actually been rebuilt in later periods.

ABOUT THE AUTHOR

Mike Salter is 56 and has been a professional author and publisher since 1988. He is particularly interested in the planning and layout of medieval buildings and has a huge collection of plans of castles and churches he has measured during tours (mostly by bicycle and motorcycle) throughout all parts of the British Isles since 1968. Wolverhampton born and bred, Mike now lives in an old cottage beside the Malvern Hills. His other interests include walking, maps, railways, board games, morris dancing and playing percussion instruments and calling dances occasionally with folk groups.

First published March 2010. Copyright Mike Salter 2010.
Folly Publications, Folly Cottage, 151 West Malvern Rd, Malvern, Worcs WR14 4AY
Printed by Aspect Design, 89 Newtown Rd, Malvern, Worcestershire WR14 2PD

Late Norman doorway at Leckhampstead

CONTENTS

Introduction   Page   4

Gazetteer of Buckinghamshire Churches   Page   20

Further Reading   Page   119

A Glossary of Terms   Page   120

A map of the churches appears inside the front of the cover

INTRODUCTION

Churches in Buckinghamshire lay in the southern part of the huge diocese of Lincoln until the creation of the diocese of Oxford in 1540. Little is known about churches of the early Saxon period in the area. They may have mostly been of timber since nothing remains of any of them. There is, however, a major later Saxon church at Wing, probably of the early 9th century onwards. It has an east apse and aisles with chunks of wall forming the arcade piers. Excavations have found traces of a possible Saxon west tower at Aylesbury. Other churches were small and composed simply of a nave for the congregation and a tiny chancel just big enough to accommodate an altar and an attendant priest, both parts dimly lighted by small round-arched windows. Remains of them are limited to walls with remains of some double-splayed windows at Hardwick and Iver (where there are re-used Roman bricks), and the nave, chancel and tall thin tower at Lavendon. Small naves surrounded by later extensions at Chicheley and Clifton Reynes appear to be ghosts of Saxon originals. Domesday Book of 1086 records minsters at Haddenham and North Crawley, but nothing standing at either place is earlier than c1200. The herringbone masonry at Ashendon, Chearsley, Ravenstone, Shabbington and Thornborough is 11th century Late Saxon or Early Norman work.

About a quarter of the churches in this book have some standing remains of the Norman period from the 1070s to the 1190s, a low proportion compared with some English counties. Windows were still usually single round-headed lights except in belfries and were set in embrasures widely splayed internally. Most churches remained as simple nave and chancel structures until the 1180s. Stewkley and Upton are good examples of more ambitious churches of c1150-75 with a central tower between a nave and a stone-vaulted chancel. Vaulting at any period is not common in parish churches and is normally confined to later medieval porches and towers. Fingest has an impressive west tower much wider than the nave and there are more modest Norman west towers at Clifton Reynes, Haversham, Ickford and Stokenchurch.

The 10th century Saxon apse at Wing

Hanslope has a chancel of the 1180s with unusual semi-circular piers carrying a blind arcade. Blind arcading appears on the tower top and west front at Stewkley and within a chancel at Wingrave. The tower arches at Stewkley are adorned with bands of chevron, a common 12th century motif. There are doorways with interesting carvings at Dinton, Hortton, Twyford and Water Stratford, but Norman doorways are less common in Buckinghamshire than some English counties and some of those that remain are plain, several on the less accessible north side of naves now being blocked up. The only tympana or lintels with figures are those at Dinton, Lathbury and Leckhampstead. Capitals carved with leaves appear at Lathbury and North Crawley, and there are scalloped capitals at Iver.

Norman tympanum and doorway arch at Dinton

The earliest evidence of aisles being added to Saxon or Early Norman churches is at Iver, Leckhampstead, Little Missenden and Upper Winchendon where were plain round arches were knocked through walls, parts of which were left to form the piers.

The chancel at Shenley with its shafted windows is a good example of the Transitional period from 1185 to 1210 as the solid and purely round-arched Norman style gradually evolved into the first phase of the Gothic style known in England as Early English in which the pointed arch prevails and arches have chamfering on each order, whilst leaves on capitals now become stiff-leaf, as at Bledlow. Several churches retain the arcades of aisles of the Transitional period, even though the aisles themselves were often rebuilt or widened or at least given large new windows later on. Stone has arcades of 1190 with scallop and crocket capitals and unmoulded arches, whilst those at Bedlow of c1200 have stiff-leaf capitals and double-chamfered arches. Joints and other irregularities sometimes show where a Norman nave was later lengthened after an aisle had been added as at Edlesborough, Stone and Waddeston.

Norman church at Upton

The much rebuilt chancel and central tower at Aylesbury   *Triple lancets facing north at Chetwode*

No fully cruciform Norman churches now remain in Buckinghamshire so the earliest churches of that type are 13th century structures at Aylesbury, Ivinghoe and Long Crendon. All of them have aisled naves. Others of that type at High Wycombe and Newport Pagnell have lost their central towers. Crossing arches of a sixth at Simpson, an nothing at all at Buckingham. Marsh Gibbon has transepts but no signs of a former central tower, whilst Radnage and Sherington have central towers but no transepts. Transepts and central towers were less common in small village churches. Haddenham has a fairly complete 13th century example of an aisled nave with a chancel and a west tower. Other churches largely of this period remain at Chetwode (originally the choir of a small priory), Burnham, Little Linford. Much of the main framework at Edlesborough is also 13th century, although the tower and all the windows are later. This church has a very good east Geometrical style window of the 1290s.

Many churches were given a larger new chancel in the 13th century, as at Iver, Lillingstone Dayrell, Little Missenden, and Swanbourne. None of them are completely unaltered or of the highest merit. The pointed-headed lancet window was the norm for much of the century and east windows were commonly formed of stepped groups of them, as at Chetwode, Chilton, Great Brickhill, and Radnage. At Little Missenden they are framed by internal shafting detached from the wall so as to form a wall-passage and there is a similar arrangement in an aisle window at Princes Risborough and again at a later period at Great Missenden. Aisles of this period are common but usually most of their lancets have been later replaced by larger windows so that only the arcades really give a flavour of the style of the period. Arcades commonly have double-chamfered arches set on circular or octagonal piers with water-holding bases, although the quatrefoil form is not unknown. Several churches near to Easton Bray in Bedfordshire have good arcade capitals, as at Ivinghoe, Marsh Gibbon, Pitstone and Wingrave.

Cold Brayfield Church: note the lancet in the chancel   *Arcade pier at Cuddington*

By the 1260s tracery began to evolve in windows by placing circles between the heads of lancets. Later on the circles contained quatrefoils and started to appear above the lancet heads as well as between them. By the early 14th century the circles are replaced by other shapes and flowing, flower-like forms evolved to create the style known as Decorated as at Great Horwood (see picture below).

The churches at Bierton, Emberton, Great Linford, Great Missenden, Ludgershall, Milton Keynes, Moulsoe, Newport Pagnell, Oakley, Olney, Quainton, Simpson, Stowe, Wendover, Winslow and Woughton on the Green are mostly 14th century work. Most have aisled naves with a south porch, west tower and a chancel, although they were generally built bit by bit to replace or extend older buildings rather than as bold new undertakings conceived and executed in a single campaign. There are good 14th century chancels at Great Horwood and Great Missenden. By this time it was normal for a chancel to have two or three sedilia or seats for priests on the south side, with a piscina further east and a priest's doorway further west. Grandborough and Quainton have the unusual feature of an angle-piscina forming part of the embrasure of a window, and sedilia are sometimes also formed in the lower part of a window embrasure.

Capitals of this period sometimes have human heads. The ballflower ornament was in use c1325-50, and the ogival arch also appeared in the 1320s. It is used sometimes to create reticulation or net-like tracery. Quatrefoil shaped piers continue into the 14th century, as at Clifton Reynes, where there are thin shafts in the diagonals, and Bierton, where there are triple shafts in the diagonals, although such elaborations were never common in parish churches, and the double chamfers of arcade arches may now have sunk quadrant mouldings, a motif also found on doorways and porch entrances.

14th century windows at Great Horwood

Haddenham Church

Nearly all the medieval churches in Buckinghamshire have towers. Over half of them were built during the period when the style known as Perpendicular was in vogue from the late 14th century through to the 1540s and which takes its name from a vertical emphasis found in window tracery and arcading. Towers of the 13th and 14th centuries were occasionally built in a transeptal position or at one end of an aisle. Newly-built later towers (as opposed to heightened or rebuilt earlier ones) all lie at the west end of the churches except for the central tower of the cruciform church at Stoke Hammond. At High Wycombe and Newport Pagnell 16th century west towers replaced 13th century central ones. There are just a dozen spires, most of them wooden recessed spires and and several of them later renewals, but there are medieval stone spires of c1370-1420 at Olney and Hanslope, and there was once another at Buckingham. Many towers have projecting stair-turrets and diagonal corner buttresses. Less common are pairs of angle buttresses, as at Edlesborough, Great Missenden and Hanslope.

Aisles were originally narrow and dimly lighted side-passages but later on they were built wider and with large windows sometimes filled with scenes of stained glass. Three fifths of the churches retain evidence of having possessed at least one aisle by the and the majority of two had two aisles. Complete new churches of the later medieval period are rare in Buckinghamshire, where the profits of the English wool-trade were smaller than in areas such as East Anglia and the Cotswolds. Only Hillesden and North Marston have a lantern-like clerestory or upper level of windows that compares with churches in those wool-rich areas. There is a small and minor example of a new early 15th century church without aisles at Cublington. Maids Moreton is a more impressive example, with good details. More common is to find a church which looks late medieval from the outside because of its clerestory, battlements, porch and new windows in the aisles, but which turns out to have older work surviving inside in the arcades and chancel arch, if not the entire framework of the building, as at Edlesborough. Haversham and Turweston are examples of churches given wider new aisles in the 14th century. Occasionally the nave itself was widened, as at East Claydon and Milton Keynes, or lengthened, as at Hognaston and Westin Turville.

Lillingstone Lovell Church

Ickford Church

Astwood Church

Chalfont St Giles Church

Splendid new porches were a common 15th century addition. Those at Great Linford and Newport Pagnell had sexpartite vaults, and Chilton has a ribbed tunnel-vault. Still more showy are the tierceron vaults in the porches at Amersham and Chesham, and the fan-vault at Maids' Moreton (another at Hillesden is 19th century). Otherwise church roofs are of timber and later medieval ones frequently survive. Most of them are low pitched with tie-beams on arched braces. Sometimes there is tracery in the spandrels of the braces or above the tie-beam. Stoke Poges has a fine 14th century timber-framed porch, and there are several other more minor examples.

The late medieval rebuilding of some churches continued well into the first half of the 16th century, as at High Wycombe, which is quite a large and fine building. At the other extreme Tattenhoe has a tiny chapel of the same period. However the building boom eased off after the Reformation of the church in the 1540s. Furnishings and monuments of the late 16th, 17th and 18th centuries are common in Buckinghamshire churches but there is little structural work. What there is tends to be a tower, porch, vestry or chapel added to an older building, commonly replacing an older similar adjunct and sometimes of brick rather than stone. Examples are a chapel of c1560 at Stoke Poges, west towers at Dorney, Fulmer, Hicham, and Little Marlow, the south side of the nave at Swanbourne, and the tower, family chapel and north arcade at Langley Marish. The classical style church of the 1680s at Willen is something of a rarity.

Gayhurst has a Baroque style church of the 1720s with round arched windows with keystones separated by fluted pilasters and with a pedimented portico on Ionic columns. A large church at Fenny Stratford incorporates a nave and tower of the 1720s. Hartwell has the earliest of England's small collection of octagonal churches. It dates from the 1750s and has two towers. Most the church at West Wycombe dates from the 1760s, although the golden ball perched above the medieval tower existed by 1752. There is also the chancel of 1748 at Fawley. The slightly later town churches at Stony Stratford and Buckingham were mostly remodelled in the 19th century.

Baroque style 18th century church at Gayhurst

Between the 1820s and the start of the Great War in 1914 nearly every parish church was restored. In some cases it amounted to little more than minor repairs to the medieval structures, at others there was a considerable amount of rebuilding and most of the old monuments and furnishings were swept away. Instances of a total rebuilding of the entire church except for a medieval tower, which are common enough in other counties, are, however rare in Buckinghamshire. Of village churches there are twenty-five that contain no medieval features or furnishings at all and thus are not included in the gazetteer. These are Ashley Green of 1873, Bledlow Ridge of 1868, Bourne End of 1889 & 1914, Coleshill of 1860, Colnbrook of 1848, Dagnall of 1863, Dropmore of 1865, Eaton Wick of 1866, Farnham Common of 1907, Frieth of 1849, Gawcott of 1827, Gerrard's Cross of 1859, Iver Heath of 1862, Kingsley of 1892, Lacey Green of 1824, Lane End of 1877, Nash of 1857, New Bradwell of 1857, Penn Street of 1849, Prestwood of 1848, Seer Green of 1846, Tylers Green of 1853, Westcott of 1866, Wolverton of 1843 and Woolstone of 1832. As the names suggest, two thirds of these places were fairly new settlements and never had medieval churches. A church at Eton (now in Berkshire) also lacks any features or furnishings older than the 1850s.

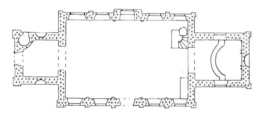

Plan of the 18th century church at Gayhurst

Detail of a Norman doorway ay Twyford

Chancel vault at Stewkley: chevron adorned ribs are Norman, cell infilling and paintings are 19th century.

Interior of Chearsley Church

Towns in the county grew slowly in the century leading up to the Great War. Amersham, Aylesbury, Beaconsfield, Chesham, Marlow and West Wycombe each gained just one new extra Anglican church, whilst High Wycombe has two extra churches and the new town of Slough (now in Berkshire) has three churches of between 1835 and 1905. Three of the medieval village churches (Quarrendon, Stantonbury, and Stoke Mandeville) are now ruins, a fourth is now a farm outbuilding, and three small minor churches (Foscott, Grove and Pitchcott) were converted into residences in the second half of the 20th century. The churches at Edlesborough, Fleet Marston, Hartwell, Pitstone and Redmund are redundant and serve as ancient monuments rather than for regular services.

A lot of wall paintings and furnishings and monuments were lost during 19th century restorations when churches were often refurnished according to the whims of the local clergy or gentry, yet, as the following pages will reveal, many interesting furnishings and pieces of woodwork have survived, along with many monuments, especially brasses. Chearsley and Tattenhoe are among the few churches with unrestored interiors.

It was the custom from the 14th century onwards for the chancels of churches to be divided from the nave by a screen to emphasise the greater sanctity of the east end. Such screens became known as Rood screens from the Holy Rood or image of the crucifixion often mounted upon the nave side of the top beam. Sometimes there was a loft over this beam for the use of musicians and the performers of religious plays. Narrow stairs beside the chancel arch are often the only reminder of a former screen and loft ripped out by Puritan reformers. Screens at North Crawley and Quainton have figures painted on the dado. Other medieval chancel screens survive at Edlesborough, Haddenham, Hillesden, Monks Risborough, Oving and Wing. Other old screens divide off chantry chapels from the chancel and an aisle.

Chancel screen at Edlesborough

Wall paintings at Broughton

Buckinghamshire is an area noted for medieval wall-paintings and those of the 1480s in Eton College Chapel (formerly in Buckinghamshire but now in Berkshire) are the finest remaining in England. There are 13th century figures and decorative patterns at Radnage, and heraldic lions and an early St Christopher at Little Hampden. There are exceptionally complete schemes of the 1330s at Chalfont St Giles and Little Kimble. A huge St Christopher and scenes from the life of St Catherine appear at Little Missenden amongst various other scenes. The poorly restored paintings at Broughton include a very rare Warning against Blasphemy. Penn has a 15th century Doom scene painted on boards and Swanbourne has unique scenes of souls entering Paradise, Purgatory and Hell. Lee also has some wall paintings of interest.

Stained glass figures as early as the 13th century remain at Aston Sandford and Chetwode. There are 14th century examples at Hitcham and Weston Underwood, plus some good fragments at Radclive and some early 16th century scenes at Hillesden. Glass was particularly vulnerable to vandalism and damage by the elements and no complete schemes remain in the county's churches, although odd fragments of figures and coats of arms remain in over thirty churches apart from those mentioned above.

Many churches in the county have floor tiles with different designs from tile works at Tylers Green in the parish of Penn and at Little Brickhill. Great Linford has a good floor of tiles from Little Brickhill dated to the 1470s by an adjoining brass. The 13th century tiles at Little Kemble are probably from Chertsey Abbey.

Norman font at Aylesbury

Norman font at Bledlow

Norman font at Chearsley

Aylesbury has the best of a series of fonts adorned with motifs probably inspired by metalwork and manuscripts produced at St Albans Abbey. Dating from the 1180s, it has foliage on the upper part of the bowl and fluting below and the base resembles a reversed scalloped capital. Similar fonts with bases survive at Bledlow, Great Kemble, Great Missenden, Little Missenden and Weston Turville, and there are others without bases at Chearsley, Chenies, Haddenham, Linslade, Monks Risborough and Pitstone, whilst there is just the base left of another at Wing. There are examples of a different type of table-top font usually of Purbeck marble at Iver and Taplow, and a 13th century example of this type at Denham.

Later medieval fonts are quite common and are usually octagonal with tracery or a blank quatrefoil on each side, often containing shields but sometimes with other motifs such as human heads or angels.

Norman font at Maids Morton

Stall with misericord seat at Edlesborough

Late medieval choir stalls with hinged seats called misericords decorated with a variety of motifs survive at Aylesbury, Edlesbourgh. and North Marston. Apart from sedilia and piscinae, other medieval fittings occasionally found in chancels are image brackets on either side of the east window and an Easter Sepulchre on the north side (see page 16). Altar rails of the 17th century are quite common, the later ones having turned balusters. The portable altar at Addington is the only medieval one left in England. Other rarities are the chrismatory at Grandborough and a vestment press (essentially a wardrobe) at Aylesbury.

Medieval pulpits rarely survive in English churches. In Buckinghamshire they only remain at Ibstock, Upper Winchendon and Edlesborough, the latter having a very rare four-tier canopy. Middle Claydon has an Elizabethan pulpit, and there are quite a few 17th century examples, often with round arches and arabesque decorations of flowing lines, tendrils and vases. Some have a tester on top.

Several churches have medieval chests in which valuables such as records and plate were kept. Pitstone has a 13th century one. Medieval doors survive at Maids' Moreton. From the 14th century onwards benches were provided for the congregation in the nave to sit on. Early benches with blank tracery on the ends are uncommon in the county. A few benches have poppy-heads and some have carvings of creatures. Twyford has a complete set of old benches. Several churches have later box-pews. Most counties have a church or two incongruously filled up with furnishings salvaged by the local squire from Continental churches, or purchased in sales in London and from other sources. Buckinghamshire's example of this is Fawley. Other churches still with good collections of 17th and 18th century furnishings are at Gayhurst, West Wycombe, and Willen.

Hopper at Waddeston dated 1736 with initials

Typical late medieval brass with small figures of a family group at Lillingstone Lovell.

The oldest monuments are 13th century cross-slabs at Lathbury, Lavendon, Marsh Gibbon, Oakley, SHabbington and Stoke Poges. Two thirds of the churches in this book contain at least one monumental effigy earlier than 1800. There are also many 17th and 18th century monuments without an effigy of the deceased. Medieval three-dimensional effigies are not common in the county. There are wooden effigies of the 1330s at Clifton Reynes and a knight of the same period at Leckhampstead, damaged knights at Aylesbury and Waddeston and a civilian at Stowe. Slightly older are priests at Ivinghoe and Woughton-on-the-Green and a knight at Twyford. Beaconsfield, Hambleden and Whaddon have early 16th century tomb recesses set in the north walls of their respective chancels, where they could also serve as Easter Sepulchres. There is a 14th century example, rather shallow, at Olney. Many empty tomb recesses show that a lot of other medieval effigies have been lost.

Effigy on tomb chest at Middle Claydon. Note the brasses on the wall behind.

In addition to the fine collection of brasses of priests and academics in Eton College Chapel (now in Berkshire) the parish churches of Buckinghamshire contain about 190 brasses with effigies, with selections of them at Amersham, Burnham, Chalfont St Giles, Chenies, Denham, Dinton, Penn, Taplow, Waddeston and Wooburn. Some lie on tomb chests and others are now fixed onto walls but the majority were set into indented paving slabs on the floor. The oldest brasses in the county are small early and mid 14th century figures of females at Pitstone and Quainton and the civilian of c1350 set in the head of a floriated cross at Taplow. A similar brass of c1420 at Edlesborough showing only the head of the deceased has now been removed. This church also has a brass of a priest of the 1390s. There are two interesting knights of the 1370s at Drayton Beauchamp, a knight and his wife of the 1420s at Stoke Poges, and late 15th century knights at Thornton and Waddeston. A mid 15th century priest at Lillingstone Lowell is represented by a heart held by two hands. Family groups from the late 15th century to the 1620s with small and rather crudely drawn figures are common. The indents of long lost brasses still survive in several places, as in the back of the tomb recess at Beaconsfield. Similar to brasses are incised slabs with the lines filled in with pitch. Chetwode has a 14th century one, and Water Stratford another of the 1630s.

Rare cross-brass at Taplow

Tomb recess used as an Easter Sepulchre at Olney

Shroud brass at Penn

The tradition of tomb-chests bearing recumbent effigies continued into the Elizabethan era, although the chests now tend to have balusters or columns on them, as at
Chenies, Denham, Hillesden, Lillingstone Dayrell and Middle Clayton. A tomb of c1580
at Chicheley features a cadaver, in which the deceased is shown as a decayed corpse,
a type more common at the turn of the 15th and 16th centuries, where it appears on
a number of brasses. In 17th century examples at Amersham, Iver and Stow the deceased is shown in a burial shroud. Elizabethan and Jacobean tombs sometimes had
canopies carried on columns, as at Chesham, Hambleden, Hillesden, Ickford, Shenley
and Wing, where there are no effigies on the tomb top, although family mourners
sometimes occur on the sides. There are similar tombs with columns supporting deep
coffered arches at Chilton, Fawley, Fulmer, Hitcham, Long Crendon and Wing.

By the early 17th century the deceased were often shown kneeling in prayer rather
than recumbent, as had sometimes been depicted on brasses since the late 15th
century, and which first appeared in three-dimensional form in the county at Langley
Marish c1600. Other examples are at Dorney and Hambleden. Effigies of this period
are also sometimes shown semi-reclining, as at Chenies, Ellesborough and Shenley. A
monument of c1620 at Marsworth is full of allegorical conceits, a theme also found a
tablet at Beachampton and a brass at Tingewick. There are classically inspired busts
of vicars of the 1590s and 1620s at Burnham and Chesham, and three monuments of
the 1630s at Datchet have busts standing free above cartouches. Other busts of that
period are at Marlow and there are later ones at Beachampton, Quainton and Wing.
There are late 17th and 18th century monuments of note at Amersham, Chenies,
Castlethorpe, Denham, Drayton Beauchamp, High Wycombe, Old Wolverton, Quainton, Ravenstone and West Wycombe. Chenies has a very fine collection of 17th and
18th century monuments in a private family chapel not open to the public.

Tomb chest at Hillesden

After the Civil Wars of the 1640s monuments increasingly took the form of tablets set upon the walls. Most of these lack figures other than cherubs or angels but they are sometimes adorned with architectural features such as columns, pediments, etc, and there may be symbols of death or symbols referring to the profession of the deceased, or even the manner of an early death. An assortment of different types of materials are sometimes used to achieve colour and contrast. Some are fine and quite complex monuments made in distant workshops whilst others were made more locally and vary in quality and size, although many have a rustic charm. Collections of 17th and 18th century tablets can be found at Amersham, Denham, High Wycombe and Quainton.

Monument at Hambleden

The Salter monument at Iver

Monument at Addington

GAZETTEER OF BUCKINGHAMSHIRE CHURCHES

ADDINGTON   *St Mary*   SP 743285

The church lies in the grounds of Addington Manor and was mostly rebuilt by Street in 1856-8 apart from the 14th century arcades without capitals, the chancel arch, and the west tower. The south aisle east window contains fragments of 15th century glass and there are sixty-two 16th and 17th century glass panels from the Netherlands brought here in the 19th century. The monuments include a cartouche with trophies and a bust of Sir John Busby, d1700, a wall monument with a putto beside a broken column to Thomas Busby, d1753, and Anne Busby, d1798, depicted kneeling beside an urn.

ADSTOCK   *St Cecilia*   SP 735301

The church is quite small but was distinguished in the 15th century by the addition of a west tower and battlements and four large windows with transoms to the nave, which has a sanctus bell-turret over its SE corner. The Norman south doorway has one order of shafts with foliage capitals, although an arch was cut into the tympanum in the 14th century. The plain blocked north doorway is also Norman. The 14th century chancel has low-side windows of two lights with transoms on both sides. It has a roof dated 1597, whilst the nave roof with pierced pendants is dated 1599.

AMERSHAM   *St Mary*   SU 958974

Some 13th century work survives in the transepts, and there is a good 15th century tierceron-vault with foliage bosses in the south porch, but the exterior was refaced with flints in 1870-2, when the 14th century arcades of four bays were rebuilt. The 15th century west tower was mostly rebuilt and given a new stair-turret on the south side in 1880 and the north transept chapel was widened in 1908. The north aisle has some 14th century tiles, the east window has some 17th century glass probably of Flemish origin brought here from Lamer in Hertfordshire in 1761, and the 15th century font with shields has come from a church at Crownthorpe in Norfolk.

The church has a very fine set of monuments, although some of them lie in the Drake Chapel which is kept locked. There are brasses in the north transept to Henry Brudenell, d1430, and John de la Penne, d1537 and their wives. Henry Curwen, d1636 is depicted in a shroud on a fine monument in the chancel, where Sir William Drake, d1654, is also depicted in a burial shroud, and there are also kneeling figures of George Bent, d1714, and his mother, d1730 (shown in Roman dress), and oval medallions dating from 1725 depicting Montague Drake, d1698. The oldest of the dozen monuments in the Drake family chapel include those of Joanne, d1625, Montague Garrard, d1728 shown in Roman dress, Elizabeth, d1757, shown kneeling with six children, Mary, d1778, and William, d1795. There is also a small brass of John Drake, d1623.

ASHENDON   *St Mary*   SP 705141

The Norman nave has a blocked north doorway and probably once had a two bay south arcade of that period, replaced by the present two eastern arches c1300. A length of walling connects them to a western arch of c1200, when the nave was lengthened and given a NW lancet. The small diagonally-buttressed west tower is 15th century. The chancel has 16th century windows and an older piscina but was much rebuilt c1807. The south porch may be 17th century. Only a blocked arch remains of the former chapel of the Falcioner family on the north side in which lay a monument of William Falconer, d1609. A defaced effigy of a cross-legged late 13th century knight lies under a later ogival arch. There is a plain Norman font and also a plain pulpit of c1700.

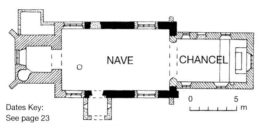

Dates Key:
See page 23

Plan of Adstock Church

Doorway capital at Adstock

Monument at Amersham

Adstock Church

ASTON ABBOTS   *St James*   SP 847202

The church was entirely rebuilt by G.E.Street in 1865-6 and a vestry was added in 1890, but the lower part of the tower with an oblong staircase-turret is 16th century.

ASTON CLINTON   *St Michael*   SP 879120

The flint exterior has been much restored and the tower was rebuilt in 1800 except for its 14th century tower arch. Both aisles appear 15th century externally but the 14th century north arcade has double-chamfered arches with sunk quadrant mouldings and circular clerestory windows above whilst the south arcade is late 13th century. The chancel with its two-light windows, a fine Easter Sepulchre with ogival arches, the traces of wall-paintings, and the chancel arch are all 14th century.

ASTON SANDFORD   *St Michael*   SP 756079

The only old feature is a much altered 13th century chancel arch. The weather-boarded bell-turret appears to date from a restoration of 1877, when the chancel was entirely rebuilt, although its east window contains late 13th glass showing Christ seated.

ASTWOOD   *St Peter*   SU 950474

The 15th century west tower has been built within the SW corner of the original nave so that the westernmost arch of the 14th century four bay arcade of the south aisle had been cut in half. The tower has an octagonal NW staircase-turret and a west window re-used from the nave west wall. South of it is a blind arch. The chancel and the blocked north doorway of the nave are 14th century. Both the nave and south aisle are embattled. The nave roof dates from 1965, the original having been bombed in 1940. The font is 14th century, there are late 16th century bench ends, and there are brasses to Roger Keston, d1409, and Thomas Chibnale, d1534 with two wives. 18th century monuments include a tablet with an oval medallion showing William Lowndes, d1775.

AYLESBURY   *St Mary*   SP 817139

This is essentially a 13th century cruciform church with an aisled nave six bays long, a big south porch with arcading internally, and a central tower with long transepts each with an eastern chapel. By the 1840s it was full of galleries and in a poor state of repair, necessitating much rebuilding during the 1850s and 60s under Sir George Gilbert Scott. The chancel lancets with ringed shafts and stiff-leaf capitals were based on original fragments. The Easter Sepulchre on the north side and the single-framed roof are original 13th century work. The tower now has plain late 20th century parapets surrounding a lead covered clock stage with a small spire. The belfry stage has twinned lancets. SE of the south transept lies a 14th century Lady Chapel set over a crypt. The chapel east of the north transept has become an organ chamber and a 15th century vestry lies north of it. By the late 14th century the eastern parts of the aisles had been greatly widened to create chapels, and arches were later put across the western parts of the aisles to help support the clerestory. These parts are now divided off as rooms.

There is a very fine late 12th century font designed as a reversed capital with scallops bearing scroll and leaf decoration and a fluted bowl with a band of foliage scolls (see page 14). There are five old misericords and a rare 15th century vestment press. The very defaced late 14th century effigy of a knight once lay in the Franciscan friary church. Other monuments include kneeling figures of Lady Lee, d1584, and her children, and those of Anne Barker Bell, d1749, and Thomas Ferrer, d1703.

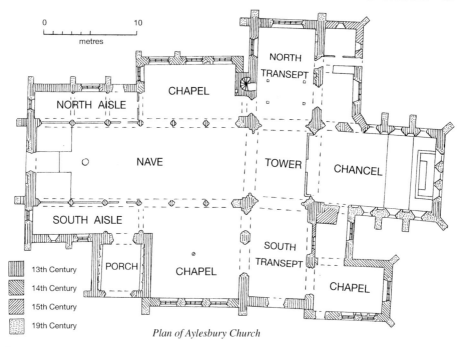

0   10
metres

NORTH
TRANSEPT

CHAPEL

NORTH AISLE

NAVE   TOWER   CHANCEL

SOUTH AISLE

13th Century
14th Century
15th Century
19th Century

PORCH

CHAPEL

SOUTH
TRANSEPT

CHAPEL

Plan of Aylesbury Church

Inside the nave at Aylesbury

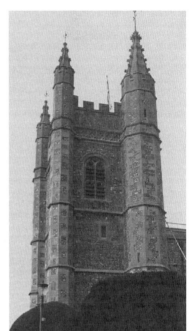

Barton Hartshorne Church   *Beaconsfield Church*

BARTON HARTSHORNE   *St James*   SP 641309

The 13th century nave has an original west lancet and south doorway and 14th century south windows and 16th century north windows. Transepts, a new chancel and a bell-cote were added in 1842-3, and new roofs were provided throughout in 1905.

BEACHAMPTON   *Assumption of St Mary*   SP 771351 ✓

The tower top dates from a heavy restoration by G.E.Street in the 1870s. Otherwise the tower is 14th century, as are the arcades of three bays with one corbel-head respond, and the chancel with its doorway. The aisles have 15th century windows and may be all of that period. Monuments include the shrouded figure of rector Matthew Pygott, d1598, a brass showing Ales Baldwyn, d1611, and her children, a plain slab to Sir Simon Benet, d1631, and a wall monument with a bust of Simon Benet, d1682

BEACONSFIELD   *St Mary and All Saints*   SU 945900 ✓

Most of the church by the old centre of the town is the result of restoration by H.Woodyer between 1868 and 1884, during which the nave was extended eastwards into space formerly occupied by the medieval chancel. Apart from the parapets the west tower with slim western polygonal corner-turrets and a larger SE staircase-turret is early 16th century, and the three western bays of the arcades of double-chamfered arches on octagonal piers are also medieval. A fine early 16th century Easter Sepulchre tomb recess in the chancel north wall has indents for brasses of kneeling figures. Another old tomb chest lies almost opposite on the south side. In the churchyard lies a tomb-chest of the poet Edmund Waller, d1687, with a corner urns and a tall central obelisk.

Bierton Church

BIERTON   *St James*   SP 836153

This is a cruciform 14th century church with an aisled nave with tall arcades of four bays on quatrefoil-shaped piers and a central tower with a SE staircase turret and a spirelet within a plain parapet set on a corbel-table. There are traces of original wall-paintings. The four-light east window is 15th century. The upper windows of the aisles may be of that period but more likely served to light galleries inserted in the late 17th century. There are rope bands on the circular Norman font. Many 14th and 15th century tiles still remain around the church.

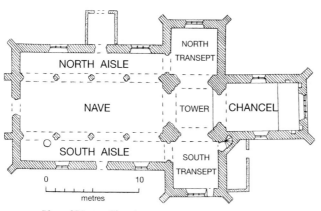

Plan of Bierton Church

Font at Bow Brickhill

BledlowChurch

BLEDLOW   *Holy Trinity*   SP 778021   ✓

The survival of a plain round-arched doorway reset on the north side, some nearby loose fragments, and what appears to have been a former north transept at the east end suggest that the present mainly 13th century structure gradually grew out of a cruciform Norman one. There are four bay single-stepped arcades of c1200 with stiff-leaf capitals on the circular piers and responds, except that one respond has scallops. The south doorway has two orders of shafts, again with stiff-leaf capitals. The tower lies on a different axis and is flanked by extensions of the aisles. The belfry windows each have a quatrefoil set between the heads of two lancets. The chancel has an east window of three stepped lancets under one arch and typical 13th century shallow buttresses. Of the 14th century are the south porch and the inner door, and a large four-light window on the south side in which is original heraldic glass with late 14th century Royal Arms. There is a good Norman font of the Aylesbury type. The wall-paintings include a 14th century Adam and Eve on the south side, a 15th century St Christopher on the north side and post-Reformation texts. In the chancel are two 18th century wall monuments designed as a pair and a brass to Vicar William Heron, d1525.

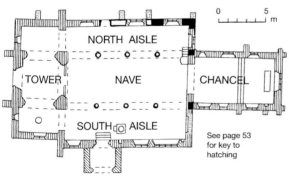

0   5
m

NORTH AISLE

TOWER   NAVE   CHANCEL

SOUTH AISLE

See page 53
for key to
hatching

Plan of Bledlow Church

Boveney Church

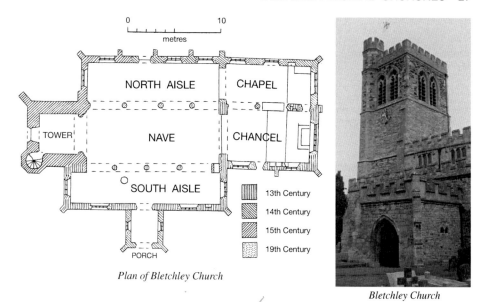

0   10

metres

NORTH AISLE | CHAPEL

TOWER | NAVE | CHANCEL

SOUTH AISLE

| | | 13th Century
| | | 14th Century
| | | 15th Century
| | | 19th Century

PORCH

Plan of Bletchley Church

Bletchley Church

BLETCHLEY   *St Mary*   SP 864339

The 13th century chancel has original sedilia and a piscina but the windows are Victorian. The doorway in the early 14th century south aisle has a reset Norman arch with beakheads and Christ's head at the top. Over the spandrels of the four bay south arcade are circular clerestory windows with quatrefoil tracery (there is a later clerestory above). The north arcade has piers out of line with those on the south, two of them being 14th century, but the western pier and this end of the aisle are 15th century. Ballflower on the pier of the two bay arcade of the north chapel suggest a date in the 1340s. The effigy on a tomb chest east of the pier is thought to be that of Richard, Lord Grey de Wilton, d1442. The chapel has 14th century windows and a later panelled roof with leaf-bosses. The aisle roofs are 15th century and so is the west tower with an octagonal SW staircase-turret. The font is 16th or 17th century and has a 17th century cover with arabesque patterns. The poor box set on a baluster is dated 1637. The other monuments include those of Thomas Sparke, d1616, the parents of the antiquarian Browne Willis (whose father died in 1699), and his wife Catherine, d1724.

BOARSTALL   *St James*   SP 624142

The windows may be survivals of a mid 17th century remodelling during which the medieval tower was removed, but above the foundations all was rebuilt in 1818, and new east and west windows were provided in 1884. The pulpit and tester are late 17th century although they have old fashioned motifs. There are several monuments in the chancel to the Aubrey family, including a late 15th century tomb-chest with shields.

BOVENEY   *St Mary Magdalene*   SU 940777

This isolated single-chamber chapel by the River Thames has a Norman west window, later south and north doorways and a square-headed two-light east window. The weatherboarded bell-turret, the sloping buttresses at the west end and the brick plinth going all round the building are more recent.

BOW BRICKHILL   *All Saints*   SP 911344

Much of the church is 15th century, notably the west tower and the south aisle windows, but the arcades of hollow-chamfered arches must be earlier and there are traces of an earlier aisle-less nave. The nave roof is dated 1630 and there are flat ceilings over the aisles. The brick east end of the chancel dates from 1756, and the south porch is of 1907. The octagonal 15th century font has quatrefoils and other motifs, and there is also a 15th century wooden pulpit from the former medieval church at Buckingham.

BRADENHAM   *St Botolph*   SU 829971

The south doorway may be late 11th century and has diapered lintel on corbels and shafts not set in the angles of the jambs and connected above by a semi-rollmoulding. The chancel and its arch were much restored in the 1860s. There is a short west tower of late medieval date, and also a north chapel once dated 1542 by an inscription now lost. The chapel east window has original heraldic glass, together with some of the 18th century. There is a brass of Richard Redberd, rector 1513-21, and a monument with two caryatid figures to Charles West, d1684.

BRADWELL   *St Lawrence*   SP 832395

The south aisle has a later flying buttress at the SW corner and a blocked round-headed doorway and an arcade of three bays of c1200 with leaf capitals on the short circular piers and pointed arches with a slight chamfer. The chancel arch is similar but seems to have been rebuilt. Upon it are two incomplete medieval inscriptions. The west tower was given a saddleback roof when it was shortened in 1832.

BRILL   *All Saints*   SP 656138

In the 15th century a tower was built within the west end of the spacious Norman nave, the west window of which remains in the tower, whilst the doorways with one order of shafts have been reset in the north aisle of 1835 and the south aisle of the 1880s. Also of the 1880s are arcades and clerestory, the nave roof and the chancel east end, but the chancel roof is dated 1637. The font is 14th century and there is a good window of c1280 reset at the east end of the north aisle. One south window has some old glass.

Bradwell Church

*Late 13th century
window at Brill*

Bradenham Church

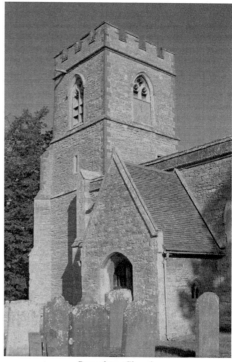

Broughton Church

BROUGHTON   *St Lawrence* ✓

SP 778021

Now maintained by the Redundant Churches Fund, this building within the new town of Milton Keynes has important wall-paintings including a Pieta of c1410 with men holding parts of the body of Christ as a warning against swearing by parts of our Lord's body. The only other example of this in England is at Corby Glen in Lincolnshire. St George and the Dragon appear on the south side together with St Helen and a bishop above a hammer and horseshoes, whilst on the north is a Doom showing the Virgin sheltering souls under her cloak. The church has 14th century windows with reticulated tracery on either side of the nave. The west tower and the large windows with transoms on either side east of the porch are 15th century.

Wall painting at Broughton

Buckland Church

BUCKINGHAM   *St Peter & St Paul*   SP 695338

The original medieval church lay further to the SW where a graveyard still remains. The central tower, (possibly with Saxon work) and its tall spire collapsed in 1776. The new church built in 1777-81 at a cost of £7000 stands on the hilltop site of the former castle. Probably the work of Francis Hiorne of Warwick, it has a diagonally-buttressed west tower with a later spire recessed behind a low parapet with corner pinnacles. The aisles are of the same height as the nave and were remodelled in the 1860s by Sir G.G.Scott, who provided a new chancel. The south porch, the heavy buttresses and windows are all of the 1860s, although the two tiers of window reflect the original arrangement to accommodate galleries. The only old furnishings are a chandelier of 1705 given by Browne Willis for the older church, early 16th century benches with tracery, and another bench of 1626.

BUCKLAND   *All Saints*   SP 888125

Of the 13th century are the cup-shaped Aylesbury style font with fluting and a band of stiff-leaf foliage and the arcade of the north aisle with double-chamfered arches on circular piers with octagonal abaci. The tower arch is of c1300 but the tower itself was rebuilt in 1893. The 14th century south doorway has fleurons in the arch. The nave has a late medieval kingpost roof. The chancel was restored and given a new roof and a northern organ chamber in 1869.

Buckingham Church

BURNHAM   *St Peter*   SP 930825 ✓

Of the 13th century are most of the nave and chancel, two bays of the north aisle with its arcade with circular piers, the north transept with one west lancet and remains of internal arcading, and the SE tower. Following a fire in the 18th century the tower had a timber bell-stage until the present one, along with the stair-turret and recessed spire, were built in 1891-2. The north transept north window and the western bay of the nave and both aisles, plus the nave roof with its scissor-trusses leaning towards the west are all 14th century. The transept is now covered by an early 19th century plaster tunnel-vault. The south arcade with octagonal piers is late 13th century. The north porch is 15th century. There are rooms and vestries of 1986 beside the chancel north wall. The church was restored in the 1860s.

The altar rails dated 1663 have come from Eton College Chapel, and there is a collection of foreign made wall panels in the north transept. There are early 16th century brasses of Gyles Eyre and his wife and of two later 16th century members of the Eyre family engraved on plates which have Flemish-engraved 14th and 15th century figures on the other sides. There is a bust of the vicar John Wright, d1594, Other monuments include those of George Evelyn, d1657, Bridget Friend, d1721, and Justice Willes, d1792.

Burnham Church

CALVERTON   *All Saints*   SP 791390 ✓

Only the three bay south arcade and the chancel and tower arches survived the rebuildings of 1817-18 (the period of the tower) and the 1850s and 1870s, when the furnishings were replaced. Two medieval stained glass heads remain in the tower windows and there is a tablet to Thomas Ravenscroft, d1752.

CASTLETHORPE   *St Simon & St Jude* ✓ SP 800446

A 14th century head has been reset over the west window of the 18th century tower which replaced the medieval one which collapsed in 1729. The nave is short and rather low, so that the clerestory on the south side is no more than a thin strip with the windows cut off by the south aisle roof. Both aisles appear to be 15th century but the north arcade is work of c1200 with a circular pier with a square abacus supporting two plain arches. The 14th century chancel has a roof higher than that of the nave and its doorway arch was once the head of a two-light window. There are two sedilia and a plain piscina. Only the base remains of a 14th century screen. Projecting heads of a lady and a man appear on the west face of the octagonal 15th century font. A wall monument shows Sir Thomas Tyrril, d1671 semi-reclining with his head in the lap of his seated wife. There is a plain pulpit of c1800.

CHALFONT ST GILES   *St Giles*   SU 991936

The 13th century chancel with double piscina and a south lancet inclines to the south. The south aisle is 14th century and the north aisle and diagonally-buttressed west tower are 15th century. Both aisles have squints into the chancel but all their windows were restored in the 1860s, when the north vestry was added. The timber-framed south porch is of 1895 and the organ-chamber is of 1884. To the west of the 15th century three-bay south arcade (with traces of earlier work at the bases of the responds) is a smaller arch under which is tucked a 13th century Purbeck marble font on five shafts. Two bays of the north arcade are 13th century and the western bay plus the nave roof are 15th century. There are altar rails of c1700 which were probably made abroad.

The south aisle contains a fine series of wall-paintings of c1330 depicting the Temptation and Expulsion, the Crucifixion and Doubting Thomas, Salome dancing before Herod at a feast, the Beheading of St John the Baptist, a Tree of Jesse at the west end and apocryphal scenes featuring the Virgin at the east end.

There are small brasses of a late 15th century priest and a civilian of c1530 with two wives, of William Gardyner, d1558, on a tomb chest, with a lady above, and of Thomas Fleetwood, Treasurer of the Mint, d1570, shown kneeling with his family above a tomb chest. There are other monuments to Sir George Fleetwood, d1620, and his wife, Katherine Radcliffe, d1660, and Sir Hugh Palliser, d1776.

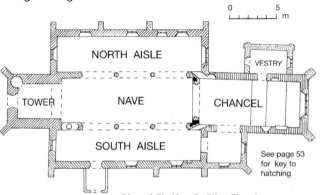

See page 53 for key to hatching

Plan of Chalfont St Giles Church

Chancel at Chalfont St Giles

Wall paintings at Chalfont St Giles

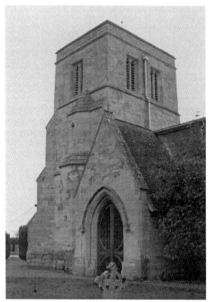

Cheddington Church

Chalfont St Peter Church

CHALFONT ST PETER   *St Peter*   TQ 000909

Most of the medieval church was destroyed when its tower collapsed in 1708. The brick nave and tower are of 1714-8 but were remodelled by G.E.Street in 1852-4, when a new chancel was added. There are some old hatchments and brasses of William Whappelode, d1398, and William Whappelode, d1446, and their wives clearly all of the same date, plus a small figure of the priest Robert Hanson, d1545, with an older engraving on the other side of his inscription.

CHEARSLEY   *St Nicholas*   SP 720104

The nave has 13th century doorways and lancets and a 14th century roof (see p12). The chancel with its axis set further north has some Saxon walling. It has a 15th century roof with raked struts to the tie-beams. The tower is late medieval and there is an 18th century brick porch. Timber framed windows light a west gallery of 1761. The interior escaped Victorian restoration and has modern box-pews in keeping with the building. The font is a late (13th century) version of the Aylesbury type with fluting on the bowl and a stiff-leaf frieze. Two windows have remains of old glass. Monuments include three 18th century tablets and brasses of John Frankeleyn, d1462, and wife.

CHEDDINGTON   *St Giles*   SP 922180

Fragments of the Norman church are reset in the nave, vestry and porch (see photo on page 34) . The chancel arch is 14th century and has a rood loft staircase projection beside it. The north aisle with an arcade on octagonal piers and the rectangular tower with pairs of belfry windows to the east and west and a staircase projection on the south are 15th century. The south porch, vestry and east window date from a restoration of 1855. There is a poorbox dated 1615 and a richly carved pulpit of the same period. Fragments of old glass lie in the vestry.

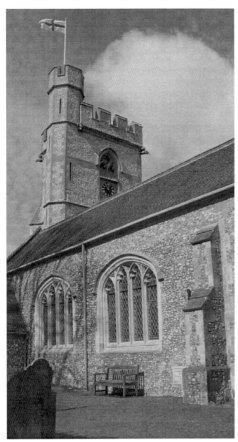

Chenies Church

Norman stone at Cheddington

CHENIES   St Michael✓ TQ 015984

The external features of the west tower with its staircase turret, the nave and south aisle and the chancel were renewed during restorations of 1861-2 and 1886-7 so the only original feature is the four bay south arcade with four-centred arches set upon piers of four shafts and four hollows. There is a Norman font of the Aylesbury type with fluting on the bowl and the ast window retains one early 16th century figure of a donor. There are brasses of John Walilton, d1469 and two wives, Lady Cheyne and her second husband, d1484 under a canopy, Richard Newland, rector, d1494, Lady Phelip, d1510 holding a heart with two scrolls, Agnes Johnson, d1511, and Elizabeth Broughton, d1524.

A four-centred arch with a panelled soffit in the chancel north wall leads through to the Bedford Chapel added in 1556 by Anne, Countess of Bedford, and still the burial place of the Russell dukes of Bedford now residing at Woburn Abbey and not normally accessible to the public. The chapel was extended northwards under the churchyard in 1861-2. A westward extension was added in 1886-7 and it was given a new east end and north aisle in 1906-7. The earliest monuments are defaced late 14th effigies of one of the Cheynes and his wife. The Russell series starts with effigies of John, first Earl of Bedford, d1555, and his wife, d1559. Effigies of Bridget, d1601 (second wife of the second earl), and Elizabeth, d1611 (wife of their son) have been transferred here from the church at Watford. Other monuments of that period are to Anne, Countess of Warwick, d1604, Lady Frances Bourchier, d1612, the second Earl, d1585, Lady Chandos, d1623, several of them commissioned by the fourth Earl, d1641, who also has an effigy, along with that of his wife, d1653. A huge marble monument to the fifth Earl and first Duke, d1700 and his wife fills the west wall. The second Duke d1711, and his wife d1724 but their marble monument was not made until 1769. Another eight impressive monuments date from the late 19th century through to the 1950s.

CHESHAM   *St Mary*   SP 956015

This is quite a large church lying on the edge of a park. It has an embattled central tower with a recessed lead spire. Much of the church exterior was renewed in the 1860s. The transepts, aisles and west front all have 15th century style windows, and there are 14th century style ones in the chancel and south transept east walls. Part of a 12th century window remains in the north transept west wall. The 13th century arcades of five bays have arches with slightly hollow chamfers set on octagonal piers. The tower arches are 14th century except for the eastern arch which may be older. The arch between the south aisle and south transept was blocked up in 1721 to help better support the tower. There a low-side windows on both sides, the southern one still with catches. The two storey south porch with a tierceron vault and a mutilated east recess surmounted by a Crucifix is 15th century. The west doorway has an original door with tracery.

Chesham Church

Two shields and a 15th century donor are depicted in the glass of the north clerestory. The south transept and aisle contain a series of old hatchments. A wall-painting of a 14th century bishop remains on the tower NW pier, but a figure of St Christopher has been painted over. There is a monument with a sarcophagus to John Cavendish, d1617, son of the Earl of Devonshire, and a bust of Richard Woodcoke, d1623, once vicar here. Other later monuments include those of Lady Mary Whichcote, d1726, and Nicholas Skottowe, 1800. Outside lies the mausoleum of the Lowndes family.

CHESHAM BOIS   *St Leonard*   TQ 970999

Some medieval work with old roofs and old tiles remains at the east end, where the window has fragments of old glass. The north aisle was added in 1881 and the SW tower in 1884, whilst the vestry and the western parts of the nave and aisle are of 1911. There is as good Jacobean pulpit and there are 18th century altar rails with twisted balusters. Benedict Lee, c1520 is depicted on a brass as a chrisom baby, and there are other brasses of c1530 to Elizabeth Cheyne, d1516 and her husband, d1552, plus a tomb chest of John Cheyne, d1585 with three shields in wreaths.

CHETWODE   *St Mary & St Nicholas*   SP 640298

The 13th century main body of the church was originally the choir of an Augustinian priory which was dissolved c1480 and given to the parishioners because their own church of St Martin was in a decayed condition. The east end has traces of original painted patterns and groups of five stepped lancets facing east and three each on the north and south (the latter over sedilia), all with fine internal shafting and also with some original stained glass figures, heraldry and scenes. Further west are late 13th century side-windows of two lights with trefoiled circles at the top. A small porch-tower was added at the NW corner after the remains of a nave extending west to the road were removed. There was originally a cloister to the south of it. A blocked arch is the only trace of a former south chapel. More remains of the north chapel, although its east and north walls were rebuilt in 1822. The pews here incorporate 17th century woodwork. Hidden under a trapdoor by the organ is a 14th century incised slab to Sir John Giffard. There is also a tablet to Mary Risley, d1668. See picture on page 6.

CHICHELEY   *St Laurence*   SP 905459

The church has a tall 15th century central tower with pairs of two-light bell-openings each with a transom. The porch, the clerestory and the embattled parapets and most other windows are also 15th century, but older (renewed) windows remain on the north side and it is likely that some walling of a Norman nave still remains, and that the tower had a 12th or 13th century predecessor. The nave west window and the north arcade with double-chamfered arches upon short quatrefoil piers are early 14th century. The priest's doorway bears the arms of Sir John Chester, who commissioned James Old-field to rebuild the chancel. It has rainwater heads dated 1708 and contains from that period an alabaster reredos, altar rails with balusters, and a screen of slim Roman Doric columns. There are brasses of Anthony Cave, d1558, merchant of the Staple of Calais, and his wife. The monument of Anthony Cave, d1554 and his wife was erected in 1576, and that with kneeling figures of Sir Anthony Chester and his wife was erected in 1637.   Other notable monuments are to Sir Anthony Chester, d1697, and Sir John Chester's wife Ann, d1704.

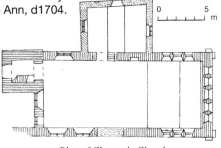

Chetwode Church

Plan of Chetwode Church

Cholesbury Church

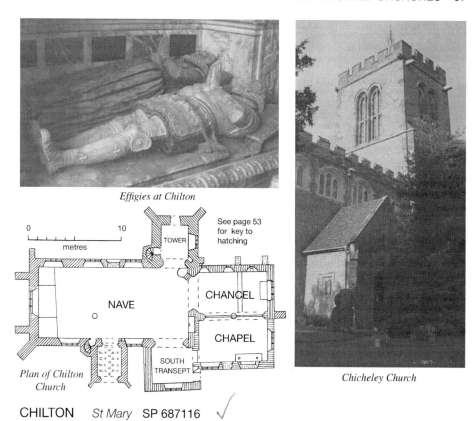

Effigies at Chilton

See page 53 for key to hatching

TOWER

NAVE

CHANCEL

CHAPEL

SOUTH TRANSEPT

Plan of Chilton Church

Chicheley Church

CHILTON *St Mary* SP 687116

The 13th century chancel has three single north lancets and a set of three stepped lancets under one arch at the east end. The short north transeptal tower with diagonal buttresses and a SW staircase turret is 14th century and the south transept is 13th century. In the 15th century a wide new nave with a two-storey south porch and several three-light windows replaced what had earlier been a narrow nave with a south aisle. The porch has a four-centred tunnel-vault with transverse ribs. The recess at the east end of the former aisle seems to have been connected with a staircase up to the rood loft of a long lost screen. The font and the chancel roof are also 15th century. The south chapel with a two bay arcade towards the chancel appears to be a 16th century remodelling of a smaller older chapel. It has a 17th century screen towards the chancel with old fashioned Flamboyant tracery. Blocking one of the windows is a big alabaster monument with recumbent effigies of Sir John Croke, d1608 and his wife. There is also a kneeling effigy of Elizabeth Tyrell, d1631, and marble screen type monument to Chief Justice Carter, d1755.

CHOLESBURY *St Laurence* SP 929071

The much rebuilt church lies within the SW end of an Iron Age hillfort and has a good 13th century south doorway with one order of shafts and a roll-moulded arch, whilst the 14th century chancel of the same width has shafted window jambs. The pretty bell-turret with a saddleback roof existed in its present form before 1710.

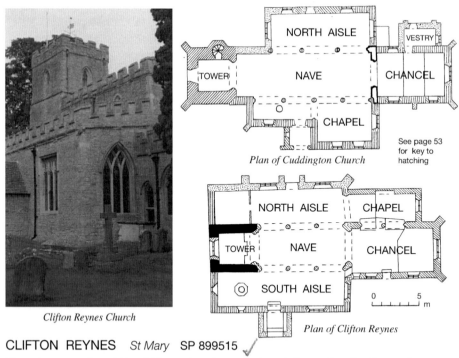

Clifton Reynes Church

Plan of Cuddington Church

See page 53 for key to hatching

Plan of Clifton Reynes

CLIFTON REYNES   *St Mary*   SP 899515

Three bay arcades of the 14th century have replaced the walls of a tiny early nave, west of which is a Norman tower with one original west window. By the 13th century aisles flanked the tower as well as the nave. The north aisle was mostly rebuilt in 1801 but two lancets remain in the south aisle. As a result of 14th century rebuilding the chancel became wider than the nave and it was later connected to the south aisle by a squint. It has original windows, sedilia and piscina and a two bay arcade to the north chapel. The tower top is also 14th century. In the 15th century the nave was given a clerestory and the whole church embattled.

The octagonal 14th century font has figures of saints and the Trinity. Several windows retain fragments of 14th and 15th glass, including arms of the Reynes family. Under a cusped recess in the chapel are early 14th century oak figures of Thomas Reynes and his wife Joan. A pair of 14th century tomb chests with effigies of other members of the Reynes family lie under the chapel arcade. One appears to have been assembled from parts of at least two monuments, and the other has the rare feature of the dog at the knight's feet being named "Bo" on the collar. There is also a bust of Alexander Small, d1752, and there are brasses of Sir John Reynes, d1428, and a man and a woman of c1500 shown in their burial shrouds.

COLD BRAYFIELD   *St Mary*   SP 929522

The nave has a Norman window set over a doorway with a chequered arch under a semicircular hood decorated with triangles. The shafts of the chancel arch are also Norman. Original lancets remain in both the 13th century chancel and west tower but there are also several windows of the 1880s and 90s. The porch is late 13th century. The small font is late 16th or 17th century. See picture on page 7.

CRESLOW   *Dedication Unknown*   SP 811219

One of the outbuildings NW of the manor house was once a parish church under the control of the Knights Templar. The last rector was presented in 1554. There are blocked windows of the 15th century and a roof with tie-beams, arched braces and wind-braces. The north doorway incorporates parts of a Norman arch with chevron and billet motifs.

CUBLINGTON   *St Nicholas*   SP 839222

The church was built afresh c1400 on a virgin site to replace an older chapel beside the castle mound further west. It has a south porch and small west tower with blank tracery in the south-facing bell-openings and a widely-splayed west window. The chancel arch sits on corbels adorned with a man and a monkey and there are castellated niches set on either side of the east window. The brick buttresses are 19th century. A brass of John Dervyle, d1410, describes him as the first rector of the church. There is also a monument to Bernard Tourney, d1681. There are framed Royal Arms of 1743.

CUDDINGTON   *St Nicholas*   SP 737111

The roll-moulded chancel arch and the easternmost arch of the north arcade are the earliest standing parts, but the 13th century arcades have on each side one pier with a re-used Norman capital (see page 7). The eastern part of the south aisle was widened later in the 13th century to form a chapel with an east window of cusped intersected tracery in which is some original stained glass. The narrow western part has a doorway with one order of shafts with filleted roll-moulded arches with dogtooth ornamentaton. The early 14th century chancel has cusped intersected window tracery. The north aisle was widened in the 14th century but lost its western bay in the 16th century. Of the 15th century are two south windows in the south chapel and the west tower with a taller polygonal staircase turret on the north side and original tiles under its arch to the nave. The porch and vestry were added during a drastic restoration in the 1850s. There is a Norman font with blank arches on the tub-shaped bowl. See page 7.

Cuddington Church

DATCHET   *St Mary*   SP 988772

Some 14th century work remains in the chancel, in which are tablets to Christopher Barker, d1599, Mary Wheeler, d1626, Hanbury Wheeler, d1633 and John Wheeler, d1636, plus a brass with a kneeling figure of Richard Hanbery, d1593. The nave and aisles were rebuilt in 1857, only to be lengthened in 1864, whilst the north transept and the NE tower and spire set over a substructure of vestries are of 1860.

DENHAM   *St Mary*   TQ 043870

The chancel has low-side 13th century lancets and was extended in the early 14th century. Although the windows have been restored, the aisles, arcades and clerestory are all 15th century, as are the roofs and the features of the unbuttressed west tower. There older walling may survive, and there are puzzling openings of uncertain date on either side of the 17th century bell-openings. The vestries north of the chancel are of 1968. The octagonal font of Purbeck marble with shallow blank arches in pairs is 13th century. Over the south doorway is a mid 15th century Doom painting. The figures include Christ seated on a rainbow and the kneeling donor. There are brasses of Agnes Jordan, last abbess of Syon, d1544, Walter Duredent, d1494, with two wives, and Amphillis Pekham, d1545, which is a palimpsest of a mid 15th century figure. There is a low tomb-chest of Elizabeth Micklow, c1550. Another tomb-chest has effigies of Sir Edmund Peckham, d1564, and his wife. There is an incised slate portrait of the divine Philippe Edelen, d1656. The best of the many other monuments are the bust of Sir Roger Hill, d1729, and that of William Bowyer, d1745, with a relief of a ship.

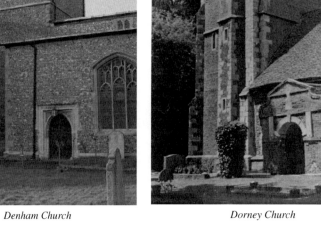

Denham Church   *Dorney Church*

Dinton Church

DINTON   *St Peter & St Paul*   SP 769110

The fine Norman south doorway has a bird on the capital of one of the shafts (see picture on page 5). The lintel shows St Michael with a dragon and the tympanum above shows two lions eating fruit from a Tree of Life. The arch above has bands of chevrons and billets. The chancel with renewed lancet windows and the five bay south arcade are 13th century, but the aisle wall into which the doorway is set is probably later medieval. A 13th century doorway is reset in the 16th century west tower. The fluting on the font may be Norman, but the upper motifs of arch-heads and quatrefoils must be later medieval. There is a Jacobean pulpit with a panel of arabesque decoration. There are monuments to Richard Serjeant, d1688, and Elizabeth Vanhattem, d1764, plus brasses to John Crompton, d1424, William Lee, d1486, Thomas Grenewey, d1538, Richard Grenewey, d1551, and Francis Lee, d1558, all with their wives and the later ones having earlier engravings on the back, plus another of Simon Mayne, d1617.

DORNEY   *St James*   SU 924790

The chancel has remains of a Norman window on each side and a pair of late 13th century trefoiled lancets on the south. The nave may also be Norman but its windows are 13th and 14th century. Of brick are the 16th century diagonally buttressed west tower with a taller stair-turret on the south side, the south porch dated 1661 with its shaped gable, and the early 17th century north chapel in which is a monument with kneeling effigies of Sir William Garrard, d1607, and his wife and children. There is also a cartouche to Jane Palmer, d1663. The chapel has windows with brick mullions. The arch through to the chancel is a relic of an older chapel here and is flanked by 14th century wall-paintings. The chancel arch with two wave-mouldings is 15th century. The interior has ceiled roofs and is unrestored. The west gallery is dated 1634, and also 17th century are the font cover and the panels from Somerset out which the pulpit was made in 1910. The font itself is Norman and has lozenges and fleur-de-lys. There are old benches, stall fronts and the traceried dado of an old screen. The family pews, commandment-boards and the boards with the Lord's Prayer are 18th century.

Dorton Church

Drayton Beauchamp Church

DORTON   *St John the Baptist*   SP 679139

The oldest feature is the Norman font set on a 15th century base and with a cover with strapwork dated 1631. The south door has 13th century hinges and one lancet and the porch are of that period. A short aisle with a two bay arcade added east of the porch in the 14th century was later given a south gable to turn it into a shallow transept. The chancel was widened southwards in the 16th century and contains altar rails of c1630. The weatherboarded bell-turret set upon posts within the nave is also of c1630.

DRAYTON BEAUCHAMP   *St Mary*   SP 902119

The church appears all late medieval outside, with late Perpendicular style windows, embattled parapets, a west tower with a stair-turret on the south and a chequered pattern of stone blocks and flintwork, and a chancel of ashlar with bands of ironstone. The chancel and south aisle roofs are 15th century and the nave roof is 16th century. The quatrefoil frieze below the south aisle east window formed part of a former reredos. Ten original stained glass figures remain in the chancel east window and there are some medieval benches. Older work of the 13th and 14th centuries appears in the tower arch and four bay arcades, and the arcaded font is Norman. There are fine brasses of the knights William Cheyne, d1375, and Thomas Cheyne, d1368, plus a small figure of the priest Henry Fazakyrley, d1531. There is a large monument with a semi-reclining effigy of Lord Newhaven, d1728. The seated figure of his wife, d1732, was added slightly later and puts the original composition rather off-balance.

Brass at Drayton Beauchamp

Norman arch at Dunton

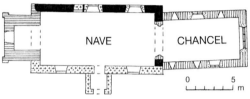

Plan of Dunton Church

East Claydon Church

DRAYTON PARSLOW   *Holy Trinity*   SP 837284

This is a small church composed of a plain west tower, a nave and chancel with 14th and 15th century features. Two sedilia remain in the chancel. There are fragments of old glass in several windows and there is a fine 15th century alabaster panel of the Crucifixion. The 14th century hexagonal font has niches on the stem with ogival arches up to the bowl. The churchyard cross has a medieval shaft with roll-moulded angles.

DUNTON   *St Martin*   SP 824244

The blocked Norman north doorway has chevrons on the arch and a lintel flanked by panels, one with a horse and the other with three figures, one of which is prostrated. The south wall of the nave was rebuilt c1790 and has windows with Y-tracery of wood, although the walling contains reset stones with chevrons from the former Norman south doorway. The chancel arch retains Norman shafts but has been rebuilt. The chancel itself is 13th century with several lancets, including low-side ones, but the roof with queenposts at the ends and a hammerbeam truss in the middle is 15th century. The small 16th century west tower with clasping corner buttresses has an 18th century brick parapet. The box pews, pulpit and west gallery are all of about the time of the rebuilding of c1790. There is a tablet to John Sotton, d1518 below small brasses of a man and wife of c1420 with inscriptions issuing from their mouths. There is also a small brass of a lady of c1510.

EAST CLAYDON   *St Mary*   SP 740250

The church was much restored in 1871, when a north aisle was added. Reset in the aisle is a doorway of the early 16th century, when the nave was widened and given a new roof and the west tower added. The plain pointed arch to the south chapel is of c1200 and the chancel is 14th century with fleurons on its north doorway and its chancel arch set on corbels with monsters and grotesques. There is a wall-monument to Elizabeth Abell, d1741 and other members of her family.

EDGCOTT   *St Michael*   SP 680229

The 14th century chancel has a transomed low-side window on the south side. The 15th century nave has an original south doorway and windows set high up, plus a staircase to the former roodloft in the SE corner. The plain embattled tower is also 15th century. Fragments of 16th century benches remain. The font is probably of c1660.

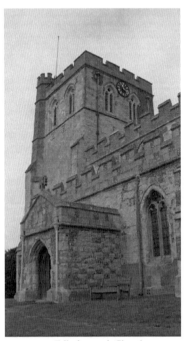

Edlesborough Church

EDLESBOROUGH   *St Mary* SP 970191

Now redundant, this all-embattled church with a wide 14th century west tower lies in a prominent position on an isolated hill. The tower had a small recessed lead spire until it was destroyed by lightning in 1828. The arcades of four bays of double-chamfered arches on octagonal piers are 13th century. The last bay appears to be a later addition after the west wall of the Norman nave was removed, and originally there was a fifth bay until the tower took its place. The chancel is also 13th century and has a fine but heavily restored Geometrical style five-light east window of c1290. The north chapel now used as a vestry and organ chamber, and the arches set across the aisles, plus the north and south porches and most of the windows are 15th century. The chapel has a five-light north window and replaced a smaller older chapel for a chantry founded in 1338. Other 15th century features are the screen and the stalls with misericords, (see pictures on pages 12 & 15) the sedilia, the plain font and the pulpit with its rare four-tier canopy. There are also some 14th century tiles. There is a brass of John de Swynstede, d1395. Another brass showing the head of rector John Killingworth, d1412 within a fine floriated cross has been removed.

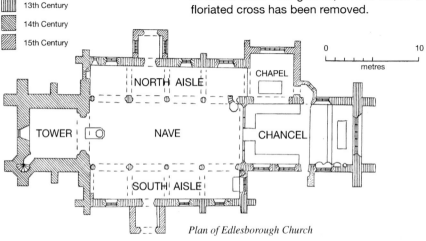

⊞ 13th Century

▧ 14th Century

▨ 15th Century

NORTH AISLE

CHAPEL

TOWER   NAVE   CHANCEL

SOUTH AISLE

0   10

metres

Plan of Edlesborough Church

Edgcott Church

ELLESBOROUGH   *St Peter & St Paul*   SP 836037 ✓

Most of the exterior was restored or rebuilt in 1870, when the organ chamber and vestry were added, but parts of the doorway and windows on the north side are 15th century, when the nave was widened on this side so that it is now out of axis with the chancel. The tall south arcade of four bays of arches with sunk quadrant mouldings set on octagonal piers is probably late 14th century. The arches under the tall SW tower with a higher SE stair-turret are of the same type. Fragments of old glass have been reset in the vestry windows. There is a brass of the knight Thomas Hawtrey, d1544, and an alabaster semi-reclining effigy of Bridget Croke, d1638.

EMBERTON   *All Saints*   SP 885495 ✓

The church is mostly 14th century with five bay arcades of wave-moulded arches on quatrefoil piers. The chancel has a moulded corbel table with grotesque heads and sedilia with ballflowers in the arches and Emblems of the Passion in the spandrels. The east window has five lights with flowing tracery, and one window on each side has a transom. The only 15th century features are a SW window in the chancel, the octagonal font with blank arches and some tracery, the remains of the chancel screen and the top stage of the west tower. There is also a brass to the priest John Mordon, d1410.

FARNHAM ROYAL   *St Mary*   SP 962827 ✓

The chancel has a small restored Norman window on the north side and a 13th century piscina. A large new nave and aisle of 1868 and a tower of 1876 replaced a nave of 1820 and a medieval tower which had become unsafe.

Emberton Church

FAWLEY   *St Mary*   SP 753867 ✓

The 13th century west tower has its east wall built over the end of a Norman nave. The top stage is 16th century and has a 19th century parapet. In 1748 the south porch was removed and a new chancel erected. Beside the SE part of the nave is a mortuary chapel of 1633 in which is a monument with effigies of Sir James Whitelock, d1632 and his wife. Most of the furnishings were made c1720 for a chapel at Canons near Stanmore and were purchased and brought here in 1747. The pulpit and lectern and the chancel panelling still remain but the nave seats were removed during a drastic restoration of 1882, when the nave was heightened, a transeptal vestry added, and the Whitelock chapel refaced and connected to the church by a new arch. There is 18th century heraldic glass in the tower, and painted on the tower arch responds are 16th or 17th century texts. In the churchyard is the Freeman Mausoleum of 1750, which a circular domed top on an octagonal base.

FENNY STRATFORD   *St Martin*   SP 884341 ✓

What is now the north aisle was a new church begun in 1724 under sponsorship of Browne Willis as a memorial to his grandfather the physician Thomas Willis. The church is of brick with stone dressings and always had gothic windows, although the doorways were classical, one under the tower having the date 1724 and a rusticated inner arch. A south aisle of 1865 (replacing a smaller one of 1823) became the nave in 1907, when it was given its own south aisle and an organ chamber was also added. There is a modest memorial to Browne Willis, d1760. He collected together the 16th to 18th century glass with arms of local families such as the Stonors and Fortescues which now lies in a north window.

FINGEST   *St Bartholomew*   SU 777912 ✓

The huge Norman tower with pairs of shafted bell-openings is much wider than the nave, which also has one Norman window on the north side. The tower has three light late 13th century west window with plate tracery and a twin-saddleback roof with crown-posts internally, which is late medieval but remodelled in the 17th century. The nave has a modest north doorway of c1200 next to the tower. The 13th century chancel has two lancets on the north side but the other windows are 15th century. The font under the tower is 14th century. The buttresses and south doorway are of 1866-7.

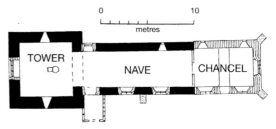

Doorway at Fenny Stratford   *Plan of Fingest Church*

Fingest Church

FLAUNDEN   *St Mary Magdalene*   SU 009988

Hardly anything remains of a church on a Greek cross plan with 13th century wall paintings. The font has gone to the church of 1838 over the boundary in Hertfordshire.

FLEET MARSTON   *St Mary*   SP 780160

This isolated church is now maintained by the Redundant Churches Fund. The chancel arch with ballflowers on the capitals and the north doorway with its hoodmould on head-stops are 14th century, and the nave windows are 15th century. The nave roof has tie-beams, queen-posts to the collars, and wind-braces. The rendered brick bell-turret has a gablet facing each cardinal direction.

FOSCOTT   *St Leonard*   SP 717358

The nave has a doorway of c1200 with a 16th century porch in front. The early 14th century chancel arch has two chamfers which die into imposts and a third resting on corbels with ball-flowers. In the 1970s the abandoned church was made into a house, an upper floor being inserted into the nave to provide bedrooms with dormer windows in the roof.

FULMER   *St James*   SU 999856

The brick nave, the north porch and west tower of the church built by Sir Marmaduke Darrell which was consecrated in 1610 all survive, along with the restored font. The openings are all of brick. Not now in its original place is a large monument with recumbent effigies of Sir Marmaduke, d1630, and his wife. A larger new chancel was added during the restoration of 1878, and in 1882 a south aisle was added with a gable over the east bay with may be a relic of an older transept. The SE vestry was added in 1961. One nave window contains four stained glass roundels made in the Netherlands in the 16th or 17th century. The original medieval church demolished in 1610 and its village stood half a mile further to the NW in the vicinity of Low Farm.

GAYHURST   *St Peter*   SP 847463

The medieval church was demolished in 1725 and the existing building was completed in 1728 for George Wrighte, Keeper of Great Seal, who is depicted along with his son Sir Nathan Wrighte, d1721, on a large monument inside. The church is a Baroque style building with the south show front having a gabled central portico with Ionic columns flanked on either side by two bays of round-arched windows with keystones with fluted Ionic pilasters between them, plus rusticated pilasters at the corners. The plinth of the whole building is also rusticated. The chancel is lower and ends in a pediment with a blank niche below it, there being no east window. On the north side the centre bay is entirely rusticated. The west tower has Y-tracery in the bell-openings and is surmounted by a lead-covered cupola. The inside has giant pilasters above a panelled dado and a plaster ceiling with the central panel subdivided into smaller panels. There are decorated cornices, that in the chancel having swirling foliage. The contemporary furnishings include box pews, wall panelling, a manorial pew, what was originally a three-decker pulpit, a good reredos with Corinthian columns carrying an open segmental pediment, a small font and the wrought iron altar rails. Over the chancel arch are Royal Arms of the Stuarts adapted to bear the arms of George I. See pages 10-11.

GRANDBOROUGH   *St John the Baptist*   SP 768250

The chief item of interest is the copy of a very rare medieval chismatory with lion's feet and cups for wine, oil and water. There is also a 15th century alabaster panel depicting the Crucifixion. The church has a 15th century west tower built of large blocks, a 14th century nave with reticulated tracery in one window and another with an angle piscina. Other windows are 15th century. The taller chancel built in the 1390s by John de la Moote, Abbot of St Albans and has several original windows of that period.

Grandborough Church

GREAT BRICKHILL *St Mary* SP 901308

The church is of dark ironstone but the upper parts of the central tower are covered in stucco. The tower and the chancel with lancets shafted internally are 13th century, although the tower top is later and the chancel east wall is of 1601. One of the lancets has some original wall-painting. The nave and aisles are 15th century but were much restored in 1867.

GREAT HAMPDEN *St Mary Magdalene* SP 849023

The church lies by the house, away from the rest of the village. Most of the windows and the clerestory and roofs are 15th century but the arcades of arches with sunk quadrant mouldings upon piers with four shafts and four hollows are 14th century, as is the nave west window. The south doorway and the lower parts of the SW tower are 13th century. There is interlacing on the roll-moulded foot of the late 13th century font but the fleuron frieze on the bowl must be later. There are 16th century benches with linenfold panels. The brass to Sir John Hampden, d1553, and his wives re-uses fragments of several older brasses. There are also brasses of John Hampden, d1496 and his wife. The monument to the most famous John Hampden, d1643, was only erected in 1743. There are other monuments to Elizabeth Hampden, d1634, Richard Hampden, d1662, and his wife, and another of 1759 to Thomas Kempthorne.

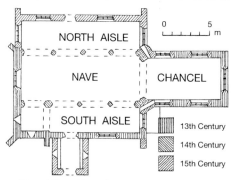

Plan of Great Hampden Church

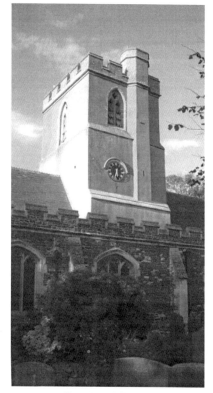

Great Hampden Church

Great Brickhill Church

Great Horwood Church

GREAT HORWOOD *St James* SP 771312

The 14th century chancel has windows with flowing tracery. One window has sedilia in the form of a screen of crocketed ogival gables set in front of a lowering of the embrasure, and there is a matching piscina. On the east wall is a head corbel. The west tower with a SW staircase turret is late 14th century. The aisles with their tall arcades and original roofs are 15th century, and the nave has a roof of that period. Beside the square-headed four-light east window of the south aisle with fragments of a stained glass Jesse tree is an image niche. Also 15th century are the screen, the octagonal font with tracery panels and shields in foils, and the lower half of a 15th century wooden figure in the north aisle. See page 7.

Norman font at Great Kimble

GREAT KIMBLE *St Nicholas* SP 826060

The embattled exterior with chequerboard patterns of flint and stone squares is all of the 1870s restoration when the early 14th century chapels beside the chancel were rebuilt. Original are the 14th century west tower and the chancel arch, plus the four bay arcades of the end of the 13th century with octagonal piers carrying one chamfered and one hollow-chamfered arch starting from angle-spurs. In the restoration these arcades were restored to a vertical position. There is a large and fine Norman font of the Aylesbury type with fluting below and leaf-trails above, and a base in the form of a reversed two-scallop capital with decorated lunettes. The red painting on it may be original. There are medieval tiles set on the north chapel walls.

Sedilia at Great Horwood

Great Linford Church

GREAT LINFORD   *St Andrew*   SP 851424

Excavations in 1980 found the grave of a 13th century priest buried with his pewter chalice and paten on the north side of the church, which now lies in a part of Milton Keynes. Also revealed were the footings of a Norman nave and chancel both within the area of the present nave, which attained its present width through a northward extension in the 13th century. This was done after the west tower had been added, thus leaving it out of axis with the rest. The tower has narrow lower lancets and partly blocked upper ones. The north porch with its sexpartite vault with a fine boss and the two bay chapel to the east of it are 14th century. There are fleurons on the chapel windows and arcade pier and one window has fragments of old glass. An early 13th century south aisle was rebuilt in the 15th century, when the nave was given a clerestory and the tower its diagonal buttresses. In a remodelling of 1706-7 the tower was given a new top and the nave was given a curved ceiling which obscures a good late 15th century king-post roof and Royal Arms of Charles II. The south aisle windows gained plain mullions and transoms replacing their tracery, and the chancel was entirely rebuilt.

The 18th century panelling and pulpit were painted light blue in 1980 and the pews were cut down in 1884 and further altered in 1987. Some medieval tiles remain in the nave (although they are now usually covered). The laying of the tiles is recorded in the inscription of the adjacent brass of Roger Hunt, d1473 and his wife. There are also brasses of Thomas Malyn, d1536, and wife, and tablets to Sir William Pritchard, Lord Mayor of London, d1704, Thomas Uthwatt, d1754, and Catherine Knapp, d1794.

Great Missenden Church

GREAT MISSENDEN   *St Peter & St Paul*   SP 900010

The church lies isolated from the village. It is largely a 14th century building with a west tower with angle-buttresses, aisles with arcades of three bays plus a fourth for transepts, and a chancel. In the 15th century new windows and new roofs were provided, plus a clerestory over the nave, a south porch, and the north aisle was doubled in width. This aisle was mostly rebuilt yet again in a restoration of 1899-1901 when a north porch was added along with a vestry complex between the chancel and the north transept. The chancel has arcading with crocketed gables on the north side, niches on either side of the east window, a piscina with a nodding ogival arch, remains of sedilia and some original glass in a low-side window. The tiles beside the high altar have come from Missenden Abbey. The tower was widened to the south in 1732 and the four-light SE window of the chancel has strange tracery possibly of that period or a little earlier. There is a Norman font of the Aylesbury type with a base in the form of a scalloped capital with lunettes and a rope moulding, although the bowl has been recut. There are 15th century brasses showing a lady and a knight's helmet with a crest with a female bust. There is also a wall-tablet of 1638 to Lady Jane Boys.

GRENDON UNDERWOOD   *St Leonard*   SP 677211

The late 13th century chancel has windows with Y-tracery and a good piscina with a cusped arch and buttress-shafts. Slightly earlier is the south doorway with broken fleurons on the arch. One of the capitals of the missing shafts is carved with stiff-leaf. Of the 15th century are several windows, the nave roof and the diagonally buttressed west tower with a SE staircase turret. There is a tier of arabesque panels on the Jacobean pulpit. The monument to John Pigott, d1751 shows him in Roman dress seated on the base. There are also monuments to Viscount Saye and Sele, d1781, and his wife, d1789 with a mourning woman shown on his, and a genius and an urn on hers.

GROVE   *St Michael*   SP 921225

This small 14th century chapel had its east and west windows renewed in 1883. The north doorway and a south window are 16th century. A wing was added on the south in the 1970s when the building was made redundant and converted into a house.

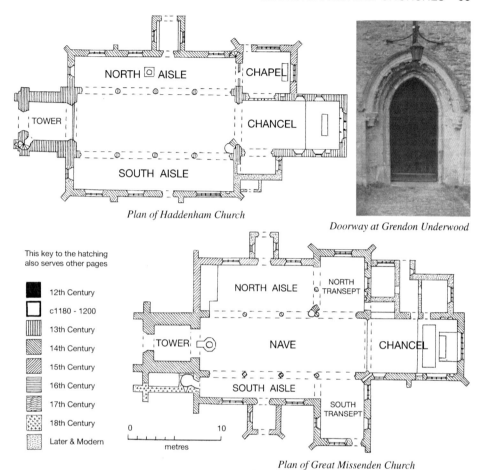

Plan of Haddenham Church

Doorway at Grendon Underwood

This key to the hatching
also serves other pages

- 12th Century
- c1180 - 1200
- 13th Century
- 14th Century
- 15th Century
- 16th Century
- 17th Century
- 18th Century
- Later & Modern

0   10
metres

Plan of Great Missenden Church

HADDENHAM *St Mary* SP 741080

This is essentially a 13th century building with a west tower, arcades of four bays of double-chamfered arches on circular piers with circular abaci, and a chancel with two original lancets on each side, although the east window is of 1864. The tower has three stepped lancets over a wide west doorway of three continuous chamfers and a blind arcade at the top with lancets in the second and fourth out of five bays. The aisles have an assortment of 14th and 15th century windows, and the north chapel has a five light north window of the late 15th century and an east window with original stained glass. The chapel replaced an earlier one of which the piscina still remains with a trefoiled arch, foliage and a round hoodmould with dogtooth ornamentation. There is a Norman font of the Aylesbury type with fluting on the bowl and a frieze of leaves and dragons above. The tower and north chapel are closed off by 15th century screens and there are old benches, some of them with ends with poppyheads, with a plough is carved on one of them. The outer arch of the 14th century north porch has a door dated 1637 with churchwardens initials, whilst the inner door is 15th century. There are brasses of Thomas Nassh, d1428 and another 15th century priest. See photo on p8.

HALTON   *St Michael*   SP 875101   ✓

A brass with kneeling figures of Henry Bradschawe, d1553 and his wife on one side, and an inscription to John Randolph, d1490 on the other, lies in the church of 1813. It was remodelled and aisles were created within the wide nave in 1886.

HAMBLEDEN   *St Mary*   SP 784866   ✓

The north transept has the unusual feature for a parish church of an east aisle of the mid 13th century. A pair of double-chamfered arches are carried on a circular pier with a circular abacus. The only relics of the Norman church, of which the central tower survived until 1720, are a font with foliated crosses in lozenge and triangular panels and a doorway in the transept west wall. The outer order of the doorway, with engaged shafts, was moved further north when a heating chamber was added. Despite its considerable length the church never had any aisles, although two bay chapels and a north porch were added beside the heavily restored 14th century chancel in 1858-9. There is also a south porch of that period made of timbers from a former west gallery. The nave has a doorway and restored windows of the 14th century. The west tower added in 1720-1 was given a new outer facing and heightened by three metres in 1883.

The fine early Renaissance panels of c1525 in the south transept altar have arms of Cardinal Wolsey and Bishop Fox of Winchester and are said to have come from a bed-head at The Vyne, where Wolsey and Fox were frequent visitors. There is also a 15th century wooden panel showing the Adoration. There are small brasses of a priest, a lady, and a civilian and wife of c1520. A 16th century tomb chest in a recess in the chancel forms an Easter Sepulchre. There are alabaster kneeling figures of Sir Cope D'Oyley, d1633 and his wife and children on a tomb (See picture on page 19), and other monuments to Ralph Scrope, d1572 and John Green, d1687. Outside in the churchyard are the 18th century mausoleums of the Lane and Kendrick families.

Hambleden Church

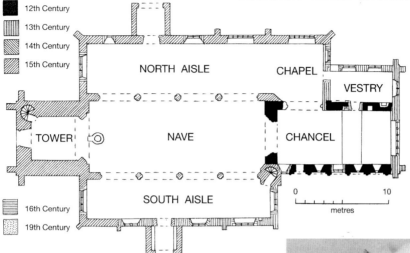

12th Century
13th Century
14th Century
15th Century

NORTH AISLE

CHAPEL

VESTRY

TOWER

NAVE

CHANCEL

SOUTH AISLE

16th Century
19th Century

0   10
metres

Plan of Hanslope Church

HANSLOPE   *St James*   SP 804467

The Norman chancel of c1180-90 has six bays of demi-columns rising up to a corbel table of heads and having between them blind round arches in which are renewed small round-headed windows. In the second bay is a doorway with stylised beakheads biting into a roll-moulding with an arch of chevrons and hoodmould of oval beads above. The chancel arch has four orders of shafts with decorated capitals and abaci. By the mid 13th century the nave had aisles of usual width for their date. A shafted pair of lancets remain on the south side, but the single lancet with a hoodmould of chevrons and a later 13th century two light window in the north aisle appear to have been reset when the aisle was rebuilt still wider in the 15th century. The arcades were then rebuilt with piers with semi-octagonal projections and a six bay clerestory added on top. The east end extends into a north chapel with a 13th century arch towards the chancel. East of it is a vestry with windows of c1300. Also 13th century are the sedilia and piscina in the chancel and a recess in the south aisle with nailhead decoration. In 1414 the rector, Thomas Knight, left money towards building the exceptionally high west tower. The spire on top reached to 60m above ground until it was rebuilt 6m shorter after a lightning strike in 1804. There is a pulpitum type screen in the north aisle in front of the Watts family vault.

Hanslope Church

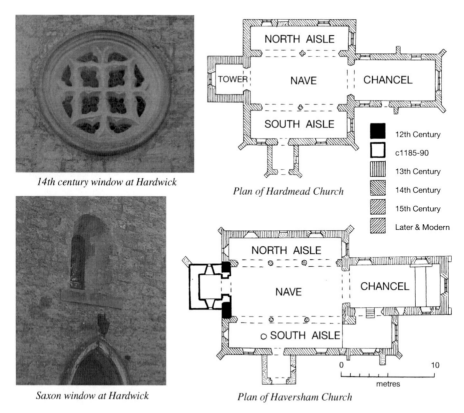

14th century window at Hardwick

Plan of Hardmead Church

■	12th Century
□	c1185-90
	13th Century
	14th Century
	15th Century
	Later & Modern

Saxon window at Hardwick

Plan of Haversham Church

HARDMEAD   *St Mary*   SP 935477

The 13th century west tower has belfry windows of two lights with a polygonal shaft between them and a trefoil in plate tracery. Otherwise this is a 14th century church with flowing tracery in the chancel windows (one has fragments of old glass) and aisles with arcades of two bays of double-chamfered arches on quatrefoil piers. Slight differences in the capitals suggest the south arcade was built first. The 15th century contributed the clerestory, south porch, tower top, the font with tracery and a rosette, and the straight-headed bench ends with buttresses at the west end. A small effigy of Francis Catesby, d1636 is set against a pattern of book-spines. There is a small brass to an earlier Francis Catesby, d1556.

HARDWICK   *St Mary*   SP 806190

Now appearing through later ashlar facing on the north side of the nave is a double-splayed Late Saxon window. The 14th century south aisle has a five bay arcade of double-chamfered arches on piers formed of four lobes each with a flat front and ogival sides. It has an unusual circular east window with tracery in the form of an ogival four-petalled flower. There is old glass in this window and in another at the west end. The west tower is also 14th century. The clerestory, roof and several windows are 15th century, but the chancel was entirely rebuilt in the restoration of 1872-3. There are several small memorial tablets but none of especial interest.

Hartwell Church

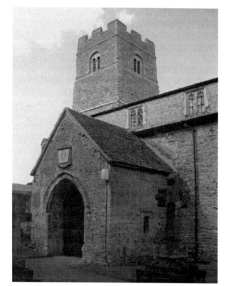

Haversham Church

HARTWELL   *St Mary*   SP 795125

Now maintained as an empty shell by the Redundant Churches Fund following a long period of neglect, this is a remarkable octagonal church of 1753-5 designed by Henry Keene. Faced with golden ashlar, it has east and west towers with belfry windows with intersecting tracery. The west tower, partly rebuilt in 1992, serves as a porch to the octagon, which has other doorways facing north and south, and three-light windows with ogival heads and concave-sided octagons as transoms facing NW, NE, SE and SW. There is an embattled attic storey with quatrefoil-shaped windows.

HAVERSHAM   *St Mary*   SP 828428

The west tower of c1185-90 has belfry windows of two round-arched lights with an octagonal shaft between them set under a plain outer arch. This tower has been added against the west wall of a Norman nave still retaining a good west window with chevrons round its edge towards the nave and shafts and a roll-moulding facing towards the tower. The chancel with its low and flat east buttresses and the north aisle with its blocked doorway and west and north lancets are early 13th century. A piscina on the outside of the north wall of the chancel suggests there was once a north chapel to balance that on the south side, which has a late 13th century arch towards the chancel. The south aisle also has a west lancet but this was probably reset when the aisle was widened slightly and the three bay arcades replaced in the 14th century. The arcades have double-chamfered arches on octagonal piers. The south porch has an original outer arch and east window but has been rebuilt. The chancel side windows and the clerestory are 15th century. One north window has fragments of 15th century glass and there are 16th century benches with poppy-heads. The 18th century pulpit has an original hour-glass with its iron stand. A female alabaster effigy of c1390 lies in an earlier recess. There are brasses to Alicia Payn, d1427, and John Mauncell, d1605, the latter depicted as a skeleton.

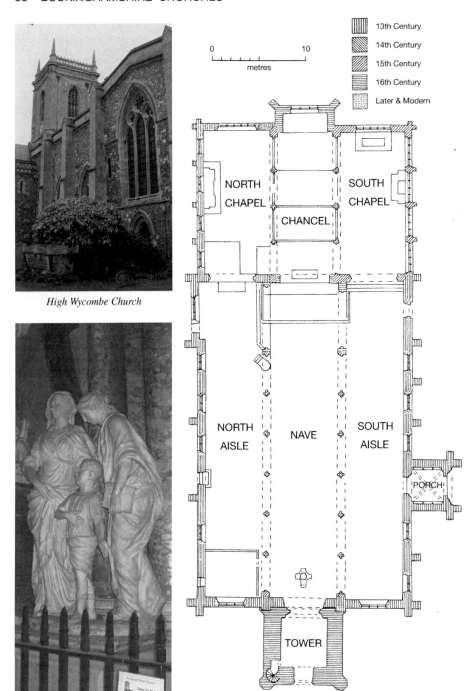

High Wycombe Church

13th Century
14th Century
15th Century
16th Century
Later & Modern

0   10
metres

NORTH
CHAPEL

SOUTH
CHAPEL

CHANCEL

NORTH
AISLE

NAVE

SOUTH
AISLE

PORCH

TOWER

Monument in High Wycombe Church

Plan of High Wycombe Church

HAWRIDGE *St Mary* SP 950059

A circular 13th century font adorned with flowers and other motifs lies in the church, which has just a nave and chancel both mostly rebuilt in the restoration of 1856.

HEDGERLEY *St Mary* SP 970874

The church itself was rebuilt in 1852, but it brasses of Robert Fulmer, d1498, and his wife and Margaret Bulstrode, d1540. There is also a painting of 1664 showing the Ten Commandments and the fates of those that broke them, plus scenes from the life of Moses. The font bears a shield, a rose, two fleurons and four heads and is probably a 15th century recutting of a 12th century bowl.

HEDSOR *St Nicholas* SP 906862

This is a small church with 17th century buttresses at the west end of the nave, a chancel with late medieval windows and a porch, north aisle and vestry of 1861-2.

HIGH WYCOMBE *All Saints* SP 865931

This is the largest church in the county and had attained its present size by the late 13th century, which is the period of the restored windows in the very wide aisles. A south porch of that era has a vault and in inner doorway with complex mouldings and two orders of shafts. Work of the 13th century also remains in both of the transepts and the north chapel, although nearly all of the windows and the outer facing of the walls has been renewed. The arcades were replaced in the 15th century by arches with a double-wave moulding set upon tall piers with four shafts with capitals with hollows between them. There are six bays, plus a seventh wider and later eastern bay replacing where a central tower stood until it was taken down in 1509. The existing west tower with octagonal corner turrets was built in 1521-34 by Sir Rowland Messenger, although its top with openwork parapets and obelisk pinnacles dates from 1755. The tower arch incorporates the head and jambs of a larger former west window. The four bays arcades between the chancel and chapels have similar piers to those in the nave, but with four-centred arches. They date from c1500 when the south chapel was rebuilt with a five light east window and a series of large four-light windows on the south.

The south chapel has original benchends and a much restored screen towards the transept dating from 1468 with an inscription referring to Richard Redehode. It contains a monument with a figure of the Countess of Shelburne, d1771, with two children, and a monument of 1784 with a figure of Sarah Shrimpton. Amongst several 18th century tablets in the south aisle is one to the shoemaker Jacob Wheeler, d1621. The north chapel contains a huge monument by Peter Scheemakers to Henry Petty, Earl of Shelburne, d1751 with figures of himself and his children, all of whom predeceased him.

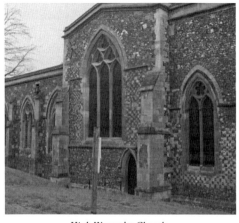

High Wycombe Church

HILLESDEN   *All Saints*   SP 686288

This is an elaborate church with an early 15th century west tower and the rest built c1495-1520 by the monks of Notley Abbey after a Visitation noted the building's poor condition. The layout with transepts and fairly narrow aisles must perpetuate an earlier medieval plan. The arcades have moulded arches on piers composed of four shafts with hollows between them and some distance above them is a continuous row of five-light clerestory windows which stop short of the taller easternmost arches into the transepts. A two bay arcade with a pier of eight shafts and eight hollows opens into a north chapel, beyond which is a two storey vestry with a crown-spire over the octagonal stair turret at the NE corner. Both the chapel and chancel have blank arcading internally. The outer walls are all embattled and there is a north porch with panelled sides and a fan vault inserted during the restoration by Sir George Gilbert Scott in 1873-5. The church had inspired the architect's interest in Gothic architecture when he was just fifteen and he had then made the drawing of it which still remains in the vestry.

Window at Hitcham

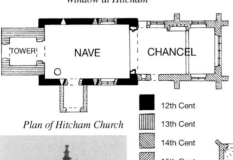

Plan of Hitcham Church

The church retains original screens to the chancel and north chapel, plus benches with linenfold panelling and one old door with traces with carvings of a sun, moon and star. Several windows have contemporary stained glass, with eight scenes friom the life of St Nicholas in the south transept east window. In the north chapel is a tomb chest with recumbent effigies of Thomas Denton, d1558 and his wife (see p18). There are other monuments to Alexander Denton, d1576, Thomas Isham, d1676, Sir Alexander and Lady Denton, d1733, and there are various floor slabs of interest in the chancel. There is an almost complete 14th century churchyard cross outside.

■	12th Cent
▦	13th Cent
▨	14th Cent
▨	15th Cent
▦	16th Cent

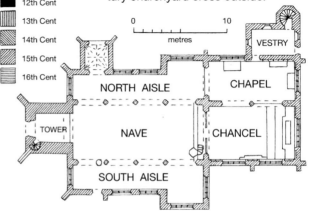

Hillesden Church

Plan of Hillesden Church

Hillesden Church

HITCHAM   *St Mary*   SP 920826

The Norman nave still has two small windows on each side. It has a wide chancel arch of c1190 with keeled shafts and waterleaf capitals now opening into a 14th century chancel with the window embrasures shafted and ogival arches to the sedilia and piscina. In the SW corner of the chancel is a circular window containing a cusped trefoil set above a low-side window and there are original floor tiles and fragment of stained glass in the windows. The embattled 16th century west tower is of brick, including the single light belfry openings and the four-centred tower arch, although there is a 14th century window of stone reset in it. The porch is of 1866 and there are early and late 20th century rooms extending north from the chancel. The pulpit and tester are 17th century. A monument has kneeling figures of Roger Alford, d1580 and his wife, and a larger one has recumbent alabaster effigies of Sir William Clarke, d1624. There are other monuments to Thomas Birsty, d1657, and George Cruikshank, d1765.

Hoggeston Church

HOGGESTON   *Holy Cross*   SP 809250

A fragment of a Norman nave south window survives between the two early 13th century arches with a slight chamfer of the south aisle. Most of the rest appears to be 14th century, when a new chancel was built, the nave and south aisle extended and the north aisle added, probably the expense of the man whose effigy holding a building appears inside. The exterior was much renewed and the chancel again rebuilt in 1882. Heavy timbers inside the west end of the north aisle support a shingled bell-turret. The south aisle roof is 17th century. There is a pulpit of c1700. There is a tomb chest with shields in strapwork to Elizabeth Mayne, d1599.

Horsenden Church

Ibstone Church

HORSENDEN   *St Michael*   SP 794029

In 1765 the nave was pulled down and a short ashlar-faced tower built in its place so that the early 16th century chancel became the whole church. The former screen now lines the existing west wall. There are many old tiles.

HORTON   *St Michael*   TQ 014759

The west tower with diagonal buttresses and a NE staircase turret is 15th century but the brick belfry stage is of c1600. The chancel was rebuilt in 1875-6, when a vestry was added on the south side and the south aisle rebuilt with transverse gables, but the three bay arcade of unmoulded pointed arches on thick circular piers with square abaci goes back to the 1190s. Still older is the fine Norman north doorway with chevrons on the arch and one order of shafts with scallop capitals. The porch in front of it is medieval, although much restored. The tub font adorned with a twisted rope band is also Norman. There is a monument to Robert Nanney, d1734.

Horton Church

Hulcott Church

HUGHENDEN *St Michael* SP 864955

Between the 13th or 14th chancel and north chapel is a two bay arcade and a third arch under which is an early 16th century monument featuring a cadaver. The rest of the church was entirely rebuilt in 1874-5 with a low NW tower, and an early 13th century font with an arcade of trefoiled arches is the only pre-Victorian furnishing. There is a brass of Rolf Thurloe, vicar, d1483. In the early 16th century the Wellesbourne family tried to prove their descent from Simon de Montfort, Earl of Leicester, d1265 by falsifying documents, and fitting the effigy here of a late 14th century knight with a false coat of arms, plus the creation of three new 15th century style military effigies.

HULCOTT *All Saints* SP 854167

The chancel and south transept appear to be a 14th century additions to an older nave. The tomb-chest with indents for brasses dates from the 16th century, when the transept became part of an aisle and timbers were inserted into the nave to carry a bellcote with a shingled spire. There are 17th century benches in the porch.

IBSTONE *St Nicholas* SP 756923

Norman are the chancel arch (probably later raised) with saltire crosses on the abaci, the west window, the north doorway with lozenge-shaped stones set in the tympanum, and the damaged south doorway with three billet friezes on the lintel and saltire crosses on the abaci of the shafts. The chancel has a 13th century east end with three lancets which are shafted internally. The oak pulpit with buttresses on the corners is 15th century. The west gallery and low weatherboarded bell-turret are 18th century. The porch was added during a restoration of 1870.

ICKFORD   *St Nicholas*   SP 646074

The saddleback-roofed west tower has a Norman window on the north side and a tall west lancet. The belfry window above has twinned lancets with trefoiled heads under blank pointed arches, although the others are 14th century. Another Norman window, probably reset, remains in the north aisle, where there is a lancet with a trefoiled rere-arch and a paired lancet. Both aisles are narrow and have three bay arcades with circular piers. They are mostly early 13th century work with an original south doorway with shafts and roll-mouldings, but with a 15th century south porch and a variety of later windows. One square-headed window of five lights on the south may be a relic of when Gilbert Sheldon was vicar here from 1636 to 1660 before being made Archbishop of Canterbury. One south arcade pier has leaf capitals of c1200-10. The chancel has an original doorway and three lancets but the east end with diagonal buttresses and a window with reticulated tracery is 14th century. The SE window also has similar tracery but with a mullion rising straight through it to a square head. Two windows have minor remains of old glass. The pulpit and the chancel dado panelling are 17th century. The monument of Thomas Tipping, d1595 only has effigies of his children against the side. Other monuments are to Thomas Phillips, d1704 and Elizabeth Phillips, d1735.

ILMER   *St Peter*   SP 769055

The nave has a blocked 12th century south doorway and a plain pointed north door-way of c1200. Within it lie the supporting timbers of a weatherboarded bell-turret covered by a pyramidal shingle roof from which rises a needle-spire. On the south side is an arch now converted to a window which once led into a transept. The 13th century chancel was rebuilt in 1859-60. Panels of c1500 showing the Trinity and St Christopher are reset in the north window jambs. Of about the same period is the screen. There is an 18th century pulpit.

Ilmer Church

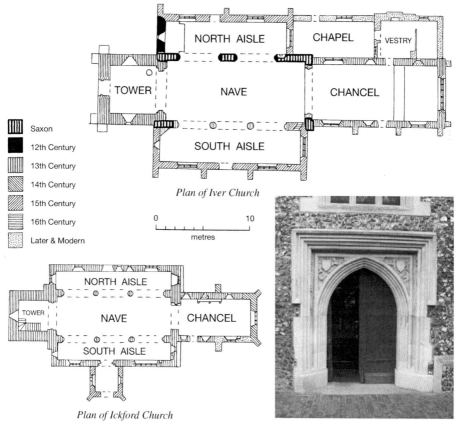

Saxon
12th Century
13th Century
14th Century
15th Century
16th Century
Later & Modern

Plan of Iver Church

0   10

metres

Plan of Ickford Church

West doorway at Iver Church

IVER   *St Peter*   TQ 084812

All four corners of a Late Saxon nave of c1000 still remain. The double-splayed window near the NW corner were revealed during the restoration of 1847. The east corners are buttressed eastwards. The west window still remains of an aisle added in the 12th century for which two plain round arches with semi-circular responds were inserted in the north wall. The 13th century west tower was given a new top stage and a new west doorway in the 15th century. The chancel is also 13th century with original sedilia and piscina. It retains two lancets, but externally these and the 14th century side windows, the five-light 15th century east window and the buttresses were all renewed in the 1840s. The south with its three-light windows is 15th century, again much renewed externally, but the lancet facing west and the two arcade piers are 15th century.

The Purbeck marble font with an incisede crenellation motif is probably Norman. There are cherub's heads and garlands on the late 17th century pulpit. There is also a charity board dated 1688 under a broken pediment. Part of an old screen remains in the south aisle. There are brasses of Ralph Blount, d1508 and his wife and children. There are kneeling figures of John King, d1604 and Anna Mellinga, d1610. A monument to Mary Salter, d1631, shows her as a corpse a shroud rising out of a coffin (see picture on page 19). The several other monuments include that of Henry Plant, d1784.

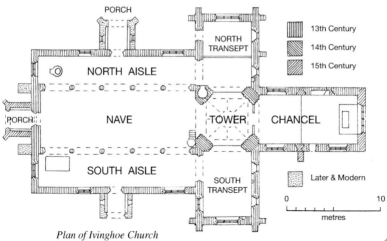

PORCH

NORTH TRANSEPT

NORTH AISLE

PORCH

NAVE

TOWER

CHANCEL

SOUTH AISLE

SOUTH TRANSEPT

	13th Century
	14th Century
	15th Century
	Later & Modern

0   10

metres

Plan of Ivinghoe Church

Ivinghoe Church

IVINGHOE   *St Mary*   SP 946161 ✓

The nave and aisles with five bay arcades of double hollow-chamfered arches and the chancel with its blocked lancets on either side are 13th century work, with stiff-leaf capitals on the west doorway and octagonal arcade piers and remains of circular clerestory windows over the spandrels. Pairs of circular windows with foils still remain in the west wall of each of the tall angle-buttressed transepts probably begun in the 1260s, although the tracery at the tops of the east lancets and in the north and south windows can hardly be earlier than c1300. The vaulted crossing and the tower rising above with a recessed spire is early 14th century but must have replaced an earlier central tower. The aisle windows and the moulded north and south doorways with ballflowers must also be 14th century. The roofs with angel figures date from the 15th century, when the west porch was added and the chancel given new windows. The north and south porches were added during a restoration of 1871-2 by G.E.Street.

The ornate Jacobean pulpit has a tester, hour-glass stand and a back panel showing the Resurrection. The lectern with a double-sided revolving book-rest and the bench ends with poppyheads are 15th century. The effigy of a priest with his head on a pillow set diagonally lies under a recess in the chancel may be of Ralph de Ivinghoe, d1304. Also in the chancel are brasses of Richard Bleckhed, d1517 and his wife, and three other late 16th century figures. There is also a monument to Deborah Neale, d1714.

Langley Marish Church

Ivinghoe Church

LANGLEY MARISH *St Mary* TQ 005796

The nave has some 11th century herringbone masonry with some re-used Roman tiles. One altered
arch remains of a north arcade of c1200, otherwise
the north aisle is renewed work of the late 14th century. A two bay arcade with a sunk chamfer on the
arches connects the north chapel and the chancel.
Both are 14th century and much restored, although
the chapel has green men head corbels and some
original stained glass and the chancel has a flat-
headed piscina and triple sedilia. The west porch is
of 1808. In the chancel are kneeling figures of 1599
showing a group of the Kederminster family with a
very rare painted architectural surround.

In 1609 Sir John Kederminster had a new brick tower raised over the west bay of
the north aisle. The belfry windows and other details are all of moulded brick. A few
years later Sir John added a chapel and private pew on the south side of the church in
place of an older chapel of which the piscina survives. A library was then built to the
west, swallowing up the medieval south porch. Although small, it is a rare survival and
quite sumptuously decorated. Finally, in 1630, Sir John provided a new north arcade
with pairs of thin Tuscan columns supporting a lintel just below the roof.

Other donations by Sir John to the church included the Royal Arms of 1625, boards
with the Ten Commandments, Creed and Lord's Prayer, the gallery in the tower, and a
bread shelf. The chancel tiles are probably those provided c1386 by the College of St
George in Windsor Castle, and the font with a head and other motifs in quatrefoils may
also be of that period. The screen in front of the entrance to the Kederminster Chapel
was provided in 1792 by Sir Robert Bateson Harvey. In the chancel is a chandelier of
1709. The monuments include a brass of John Bowser, d1608, a woman leaning on a
pedestal and urn for David Harvey, d1788, and an obelisk for Robert Gosling, d1794.

Lathbury Church

LATHBURY   *All Saints*   SP 875450

The nave is Norman and has one original window remaining above the south arcade. With it goes a fragment of a doorway tympanum of c1100 now reset in the nave NE corner on which is a Tree of Life and two beasts. The south aisle of c1200 has a doorway of two orders with leaf responds and nailheads on the hood. The arcade of the same period has dragons on the capital of the circular pier carrying two pointed arches with a slight chamfer. The aisle east window with bar-tracery is later 13th century and the larger south windows with intersecting tracery cannot be earlier than c1300. A north aisle was then added and a new chancel with windows with flowing tracery and a double piscina and sedilia with ogival cusping which cannot be earlier than the 1330s. One south window has a mouchette wheel for tracery and fragments of old glass. The low clerestory and the ironstone battlements are 15th century. The west tower with belfry windows with arches over twin lancets divided by an octagonal shaft is early 13th century, but the tower arch dates only from the restoration of 1869.

The chancel has a black and white marble pavement which was donated in the late 17th century by Margaret, daughter of Sir Henry Andrewes. Fragments remain of wall paintings of c1510 and earlier showing a Doom over the chancel arch, a Weighing of Souls over the north arcade, a Heavenly Jerusalem, and Works of Mercy including Burying the Dead over the south arcade. There are also post-Reformation texts. There is a monument to Henry Uthwatt, d1757, and also a worn 13th century cross-slab.

LATIMER   *St Mary Magdalene*   TQ 001989

From the former medieval chapel here have come a Jacobean pulpit and a monument to Anna Wortley, d1632, now lying in the new church of 1841 mostly rebuilt and much extended in 1867.

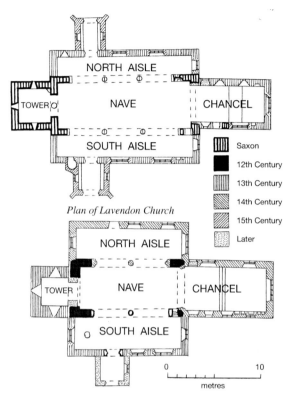

Plan of Lavendon Church

Saxon	
12th Century	
13th Century	
14th Century	
15th Century	
Later	

Plan of Lathbury Church

Lavendon Church

LAVENDON   *St Mary*   SP 916537

Of a Late Saxon church there remain all four corners of the nave, plus walling above the arcades, part of the south wall of the chancel, which inclines to the south, and the tall west tower with several windows built without cut stone and some herringbone-masonry. Over the blocked priest's doorway is the head of another Saxon window and yet another is cut into by the east bay of the north arcade. Both the aisles and their three bay arcades with circular piers are early 13th century, and one small lancet remains on the north side. Two more lancets remain in the chancel north wall. The east window and the bracket with a bearded head are 14th century. Of the 15th century are the tower top stage, the clerestory, the three light aisle windows and north and south porches. Reset on the latter is a 13th century grave-slab with a floriated cross. The furnishings date from the restoration of 1858-9 except for the Jacobean pulpit and the 15th century font with tracery patterns and a fleur-de-lis.

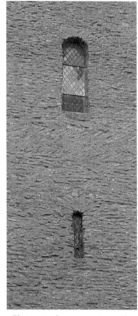

Close up of tower at Lavendon

LECKHAMPSTEAD *Assumption of the Virgin* SP 727380

The Norman south doorway probably of c1150-60 has shafts adorned with scales and chevrons and capitals showing birds with outstretched wings looking downwards. The arch has a thick roll-moulding. The tympanum with two intertwined dragons with a demon and a row of saltire crosses below may be older work re-used. An early 16th century porch repaired in 1688 now stands in front. The thinner walling west of the porch may date from the 1190s when a north aisle was added with an arcade of square piers carrying pointed arches with on the nave side a hoodmould in the form of a band with lunettes cut out both sides. The restored north doorway has leaves in the spandrels and chevrons on the hoodmould. One arcade pier has a 13th century inscription referring to Isabella's seat, a rare piece of evidence that churches had seats by then. The west tower is 13th century but has later battlements and a pyramidal roof. The chancel is 14th century but has been restored, and the round-headed sedilia look 16th century. The octagonal font carved with the Crucifixion, a bishop, St Catherine and a Virgin and Child looks 14th century, but could be a Norman bowl later recut. There is an effigy of a knight of c1325. There are also brasses of Reginald Tylney, d1506, and of a lady of the same period.

LEE *Dedication Unknown* SP 897044

This tiny 13th century chapel has several original lancets, including a group of three under one arch in the east wall, and one window has fragments of old glass, but its main interest lies in the wall paintings. They include St George and the Dragon and a Weighing of Souls on the west wall, and St Christopher on the north wall. There are minor memorials of the 18th and 19th centuries to members of the Deering family.

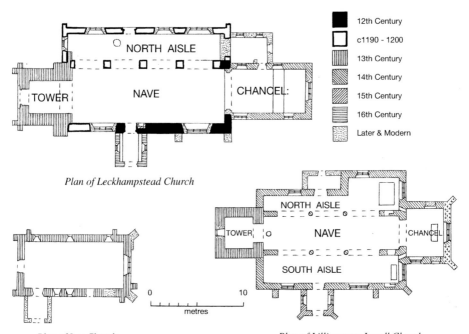

■	12th Century
□	c1190 - 1200
▦	13th Century
▧	14th Century
▨	15th Century
▤	16th Century
▒	Later & Modern

Plan of Leckhampstead Church

Plan of Lee Church

Plan of Lillingstone Lovell Church

Leckhampstead Church

LILLINGSTONE DAYRELL   *St Nicholas*   SP 706398

The plain chancel arch is Early Norman. The tower arch seems later Norman but the tower itself with twinned lancets at the belfry stage is clearly 13th century. The 13th century chancel has arcading on the inside of the south wall, a lowside SW window a SE window with dogtooth and a tomb recess cum Easter Sepulchre in the north wall. The east window of c1280 has three stepped lancets, shafted internally, with three foiled circles above. The three bay arcades and the good south doorway with one order of shafts are also later 13th century. The north aisle was rebuilt in 1868 when a vestry and organ chamber were added, but the south aisle has 14th century windows and a tiny 15th century stone-roofed porch. In the chancel are medieval tiles and a cross from a gable of the building. Effgies of Paul Dayrell and his wife of 1571 lie on a tomb chest, and brasses of another Paul Dayrell, d1491 and his wife lie on another tomb chest. There is also a small mutilated brass of the priest Richard Blakysley, d1493.

LILLINGSTONE LOVELL   *Assumption of the Virgin*   SP 713405

The re-set south doorway or two orders with leaf capitals and the west tower are 13th century, although the belfry windows are 14th century. During that century the tiny original nave was lengthened eastwards and given aisles with three bay arcades, the west responds having heads. The north aisle is narrow except for the east bay with is twice the width to form a chapel which retains fragment of old glass in its east window. Each aisle has a double piscina and a squint through to a wider new chancel added beyond the extension. It was shortened in 1777 when the original east window was reset in a new wall. The south porch of 1639 was mostly rebuilt in 1891-2, when the clerestory and north vestry were added. The rededos, altar rails and the Commandments over the altar are all early 18th century, as are the box-pews. The pulpit is Jacobean. The brass of John Merstun, rector, d1446 shows just two hands holding a heart. Other brasses depict Thomas Clarell, d1471, and William Rysley, d1516 and their wives. There are also two good late 18th century monuments to the Wentworths.

LITTLE BRICKHILL   *St Mary Magdalene*   SP 911325

The oldest features are the 14th century chancel arch with trefoils beside the capitals and the blocked arch of a former north transept which collapsed in a storm in 1703. Browne Willis had the chancel repaired after that storm but it was mostly rebuilt in 1864-5 along with the upper part of the 15th century tower which is oddly offset to the north. The four bay south arcade and the arch to the south chapel, plus the outer arch of the south porch all look like work of c1600. The chapel has an old piscina.

LITTLE HAMPDEN   *Dedication Unknown*   SP 860035

The chancel has one renewed lancet with a transom and the nave must also go back to at least the 13th century since it has wall paintings of that period including a row of saints under trefoil-headed arches, St Peter and St Paul, St Christopher and a Weighing of Souls with the Virgin sheltering souls under her cloak. The south and west windows are 18th century but there is a 15th century roof with cambered tie-beams, curved braces to the collar and tall crown-posts. The short timber-framed porch tower on the north side is also 15th century.

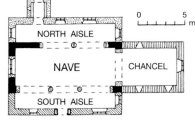

Plan of Little Linford Church

Wall painting at Little Kimble

Little Brickhill Church

LITTLE HORWOOD   *St Nicholas*   SP 791309

The four bay arcades are 13th century but differing stone colours and unequal widths of bays suggest later rebuilding and possibly heightening. The early 14th century chancel arch is out of axis with the rest of the church. The south aisle seems to have been lengthened eastwards and probably rebuilt in the 15th century. The porch is of 1828 and there is a Jacobean pulpit. Various layers of wall paintings going back to the late 13th or early 14th century were discovered on the north wall in 1899 when the exterior was mostly renewed except for the 15th century west tower of large ashlar blocks. On the nave east wall is a brass plate of 1641 with the Ten Commandments.

LITTLE KIMBLE   *All Saints*   SP 826065

The exterior was much restored in 1847 but the chancel has windows of c1300 and one nave window retains some 14th century glass. Of greater interest are the 13th century tiles depicting knights and a king on his throne brought here from Chertsey Abbey, and the fine series of 14th century wall paintings. There are figures of St James, St Christopher, a bishop holding a building, St George, St Lawrence, the martyrdom of St Margaret, the burial of St Catherine, St Francis preaching to birds and a devil pushing two women headfirst into the mouth of Hell.

LITTLE LINFORD   *St Leonard*   SP 847442

The north aisle is entirely of 1878 with a porch of that period and replaced a long-lost 13th century aisle of which the two bay arcade still remains with a circular pier with an octagonal abacus. The plain double bellcote is 13th century. Much of the chancel is of 1896 but the two light east window with a quatrefoil in plate tracery is original late 13th century work. The south aisle has two windows and an arcade of the 14th century but also a Norman doorway with chevrons on the hoodmould. Of the 15th century are the west window, the roof with cambered tie-beams with arched braces, and fragments of a screen re-used in the altar table. There are 17th or 18th century communion rails and a Norman font. There are two matching memorial medallions to members of the Knapp family, Matthew, d1782 and Sophia d1795.

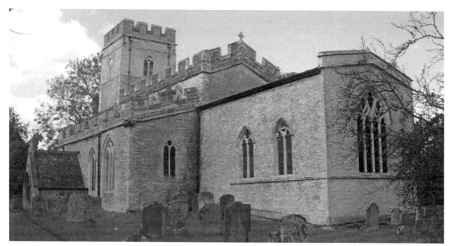

Little Linford Church

Little Marlow Church

Window at Little Marlow

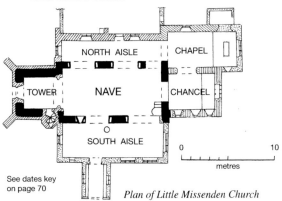

See dates key
on page 70

Plan of Little Missenden Church

LITTLE MARLOW   *St John the Baptist*   SP 874879   ✓

There is a round Norman arch between the chancel and the south chapel. The plain pointed chancel arch may also be no later than c1200. The chancel has good north windows with Geometrical tracery of two lights with a sexfoiled circle above dating from c1275 (see picture above). The nave has a reset piscina of that period with a trefoiled head and dogtooth ornamentation. The chancel east window with a vertical form of reticulation and fragments of old glass is late 14th century. The north arcade with two sunk quadrants on the arches is 14th century, whilst the south arcade with one sunk quadrant and one hollow chamfer is probably 15th century. The west tower is 14th century but the pairs of simple belfry windows are 16th century. All the roofs contain old woodwork but the nave dormer windows are 20th century replacements of 17th century originals. There is a plain Norman font. The south chapel was probably built by Alice and Nicholas Ledewich, whose tomb of c1430 flanks the sanctuary. A brass showing her still remains. There is also a monument to James Chase, d1721.

Tower at Little Missenden   *Early arcade and wall paintings at Little Missenden*

LITTLE MISSENDEN   *St John the Baptist*   SU 921990

The plain chancel arch with flat imposts of Roman brick dates from c1100. The west tower is thought to be a 15th century remodelling of a Norman structure and the walls of the early nave partly survive too. In the 12th century two plain round arches were made through the south wall for an aisle and a clerestory added, one blocked window of which remains, now cut into by the 15th century roof. Later on in the 12th century two more arches (out of line with the others) were made in the north wall, the responds this time having nook-shafts. The aisle itself was rebuilt in the 15th century. The south aisle was rebuilt in brick in the 18th century, although the south doorway and parts of the porch are 15th century. The small chancel has single lancets facing south and a shafted triplet of them facing east. The early 14th century north chapel extends further east. The dormer window in the nave roof existed by 1777 and may be 17th century.

A tomb recess in the chapel has old tiles. There is a Norman font of the Aylesbury type with the lower half fluted and the upper half with three-lobed leaves. There are many wall paintings, including a St Christopher and the 14th century martyrdom of St Catherine on the north wall, a Crucifixion below on a pier, and 13th century foliage on the chancel arch and the Annunciation to the Shepherds in the chapel. Fragmentary Tudor Royal Arms remain over the chancel arch, having replaced a Doom of c1400. There are also many post-Reformation texts.

LITTLE WOOLSTONE   *Holy Trinity*   SP 876386

The 14th century nave with windows with reticulated tracery now forms a community centre for a Milton Keynes suburb, and its kingpost roof is ceiled below the collar. The chancel as rebuilt and given a north vestry in 1861 still serves as a chapel. The church was declared redundant in 1969 and in 1980 excavations found evidence of a much earlier and smaller nave to which was later added a side chapel. Some old tiles remain and also a Norman font with intersecting arches and chevron band at the top.

LONG CRENDON   *St Mary*   SP 699091   ✓

This is a cruciform church with a tall late 15th century central tower with pairs of two-light belfry windows with transoms and a higher NW stair-turret. However, the arches below it are 13th century, as is most of the church, with lancets still remaining in the north transept east wall and on both sides of the chancel, and a good south doorway with one order of shafts in the south aisle. The arcades are of just two wide bays, with an octagonal pier on the south and a quatrefoil one on the north. Still earlier is the west end of the nave where a Norman window head remains above where there is 16th century arcaded walling with a porch in front of it. In the 14th century the north aisle was widened and given a porch and a fine internal niche, whilst the north transept was given a new north wall with a spectacular window with five lights rising to a ten-spoked wheel. The south porch, one south window and most of the south transept are 15th century. Also of that period are the chancel roof with a tracery-frieze above the wall-plate and collar beams on arch braces, and also the font with seated lions by the foot, frontal heads in quatrefoils and half-figures of angels. In the 1630s the transept south window was blocked by a monument with recumbent effigies of Sir John Dormer and his wife, but two new windows were made in the east wall instead and some work done on the tower piers. The main west window is also probably of that period. The only other memorial of note is a brass to John Canon, d1460 and his wife. The altar rails and north transept screens are Jacobean and there is a slightly later and grander south transept screen. A few medieval tiles remain in the chancel.

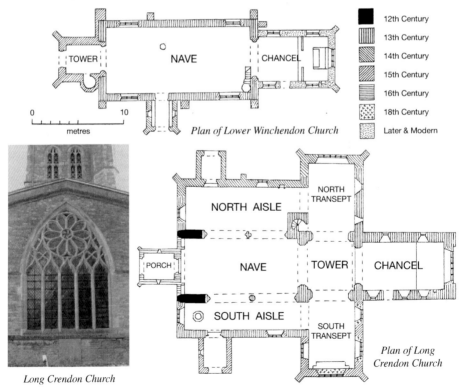

■	12th Century
▥	13th Century
▧	14th Century
▨	15th Century
▤	16th Century
▦	18th Century
▨	Later & Modern

TOWER   NAVE   CHANCEL

0   10
metres

Plan of Lower Winchendon Church

NORTH AISLE

NORTH TRANSEPT

PORCH   NAVE   TOWER   CHANCEL

SOUTH AISLE

SOUTH TRANSEPT

Plan of Long Crendon Church

Long Crendon Church

LOUDWATER   *St Peter*   SU 900905

The brick nave was built as a chapel-of-ease in 1788 to a design by William Davis, who also paid for the work. The hipped roofed south and north projections with arched windows and lunettes are of 1804 and 1835 respectively. The east end is of 1903-4 and there is a modern west porch.

LOUGHTON   *All Saints*   SP 837379

The nave and chancel are of uncertain date, but the blocked north doorway and the tall lancet are probably 14th century. The diagonally buttressed west tower is 15th century Of the end of that century are the south aisle and chapel with an older porch incorporated at the west end. It has an arcade of double-chamfered arches on octagonal piers and some old parts in the roof. There is a small demi-figure of a priest of c1510.

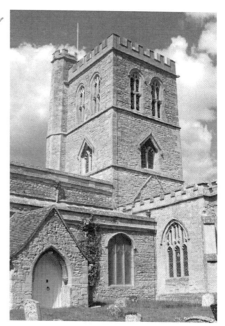

Long Crendon Church

LOWER WINCHENDON   *St Nicholas*   SP 764144

The diagonally-buttressed west tower with a higher stair-turret is 15th century, as are the windows and buttresses of the nave. The walling, however is older since there is a 14th century south porch and the chancel arch is late 13th century. The chancel was rebuilt in 1891. Two windows have some old glass and here is a Jacobean pulpit dated 1613 with a small tester. The pews, west gallery and roof are of the 1820s. There are brasses of John Hampden, d1420 and John Barton, d1487 and their wives.

Lower Winchedon Church

Ludgershall Church

Sedilia at Maids' Morton

LUDGERSHALL *St Mary* SP 660172

The nave and narrow aisles with four bay arcades of double-chamfered arches and also the chancel arch are 14th century, the east window in the north aisle having some flowing tracery and original stained glass. There are human busts on the piers, with interlocking arms on one on the south side. The aisles have squints through to the chancel, which has a 14th century piscina and may be structurally of that date, together with the bellcote over the chancel arch, although its windows and hammer-beam roof with pendants are 15th century. Also 15th century are the two-storey south porch and the tower inserted into the western bay of the nave. The low pitched nave roof with tie-beams and figures holding shields, and the windows of the south aisle (and one on the north) are 16th century. The chancel east window and organ chamber are of 1889. There is a Norman font with fluting with foliage below. On a tomb chest are brasses of Anne Englishe, d1565 with two other women.

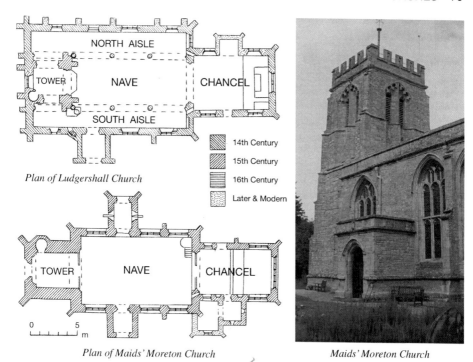

Plan of Ludgershall Church

14th Century
15th Century
16th Century
Later & Modern

0   5
     m

Plan of Maids' Moreton Church

Maids' Moreton Church

MAIDS' MORETON   *St Edmund*   SP 707351

Although it contains a Norman font with a band of leaf patterns, the whole building itself is all mid 15th century and according to a later inscription was sponsored by two maiden sisters of the Peover family of Toddington. Brasses of them dating from 1890 are set in original indents. Their church has a wide nave of four bays with three light windows with panel tracery and transoms extending downwards internally as blankl arcading. A squint on the south side leads through to the chancel which has a good east window of five lights with three transoms. There are three fine sedilia with a 16th century wall painting of the Last Supper on the back. Doorways with porches with fan-vaults open onto the second bay from the west and there are other fan-vaults over the vestry beside the chancel and under the tower. The tower has very peculiar belfry windows with a single light set either side of a V-shaped buttress rising to the head of a finely cusped arch. There is a similar motif in the north porch. The parapet merlons are pierced by small circular holes. The date 1637 with the Peover Arms appears on the north door, and the outer porch entrance was altered at that time. Both of the main roofs are partly original and several windows have fragments of original glass. There is a cartouche to Frances Attenbury, d1685, and a good tablet to Edward Bate, d1717.

MARLOW   *All Saints*   SP 851861

The church was rebuilt in 1832-5, but much remodelled with a new chancel and new arcades in 1875-6 and 1881-2. The monuments include those of Katheryne Willough-by, d1597, Richard Davenport, d1799, and Sir Miles Hobart, d1632, whose tablet has a scene of the coach accident that killed him nearby at Holborn.

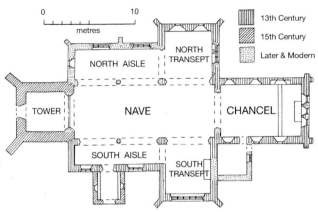

Plan of Marsh Gibbon Church

Marsh Gibbon Church

MARSH GIBBON   *St Mary*   SP 648232

This is a cruciform church mostly dating from the 13th century with a good foliated cross-slab of that period. However the clerestory, south porch, west tower and several windows make the building look of c1500 externally, and there was some renewing of the chancel lancets in 1860. Original lancets remain in the north transept and another was reset in west end of the north aisle when it was added in 1880. The arcades have two wide bays to each aisle and a third wider bay to the transepts, without any evidence there was ever a central tower. The capitals have stiff-leaves and one also has some grapes. The south transept has a large south window of five lights with panel-tracery. There are plain 17th century benches.

Marsworth Church

MARSWORTH   *All Saints*   SP 920146

In the 14th century the chancel was rebuilt and a north aisle and chapel added, with arcades of three and two bays respectively. A west tower was added to the aisle in the 15th century and these northern parts have now become the nave and chancel and the original parts have become the aisle and chapel. The chequer work of flint and stone on the south side dates from the heavy restoration of 1882-91. The pulpit sits on a big 14th century capital with angels and foliage. A brass has effigies of Nicholas West, d1586 and his wife on one side and a large and finely robed late 15th century German priest on the other. A rare scene of Christ risen appears on the tomb chest of Edmund West, d1618, which also has allegorical reliefs of skulls and Death with a scythe.

Marsh Gibbon Church

MEDMENHAM   *St Peter*   SP 805845

Much of the exterior walling may be 16th or 17th century and there was a heavy restoration in the 1840s, which swept away older monuments and furnishings, but plain late 12th century doorways survive on both sides, although the northern one is blocked. A 13th century arch opens into a north transept of 1925 replacing a transept or chapel demolished c1720. The 15th century west tower was rendered in 1987.

MENTMORE   *St Mary*   SP 904198

In 1858 the chancel and aisles were rebuilt, the vestry added and the west tower refaced. The three bay arcades and the clerestory and parts of the roof with angels survive from the late 14th century. The pier bases are re-used circular capitals of c1200 with waterleaf, and the quatrefoil piers may also be cut-down circular piers. One window has fragments of old glass and there is an Italian relief of the Virgin and Child.

Medmenham Church

MIDDLE CLAYDON   *All Saints*   SP 719253

The church lies close to the house and contains brasses of Isabella Giffard, d1523, Roger Giffard, d1542 and his wife, and the priest Alexander Anne, d1526. A recumbent effigy of Margaret Giffard, d1539 lies on a tomb chest (see page 16). A large monument has busts of Sir Edmund Verney, d1642, and his wife and son and daughter-in-law. Other Verney monuments include those of Henry, d1671, Elizabeth, d1694, and Mary, d1694. An inscription refers to the rebuilding of the chancel in 1519. The screen is of that period, and perhaps also the west tower. Most of the features of the nave and chancel date from a restoration of 1870 but a recess (now a doorway) in the chancel south wall has demi-figures of angels under the arch. There is an Elizabethan pulpit.

MILTON KEYNES   *All Saints*   SP 888391

This is the church of the original village of Milton Keynes. The wide nave with a south porch and north transeptal tower plus the chancel and north chapel with a two bay arcade with a circular pier with a round abacus are all 14th century. The belfry windows have intersecting tracery and the tower arch has ballflowers. The chapel has two low-side windows with modern shutters and ballflowers on the piscina. The chancel piscina forms part of a group with sedilia and a credence shelf. There is a third piscina in the tower, where the lower stage with blind arches must have been a chapel. The only earlier parts are a reset outer opening of a lancet in the nave and the chancel arch of c1200 with leaf capitals. Its position shows that the nave is wider than the Norman one was and probably includes the width of a former north aisle. A few old tiles remain in the chancel and there is a brass of the priest Adam Babyngton, d1427.

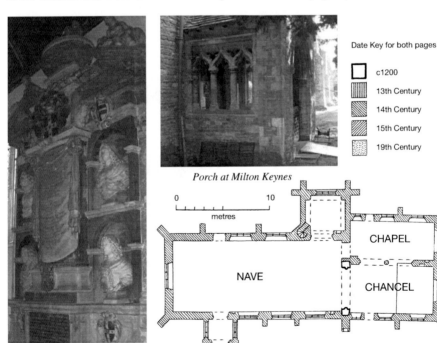

Porch at Milton Keynes

Date Key for both pages

☐ c1200

▦ 13th Century

▨ 14th Century

▨ 15th Century

▦ 19th Century

0   10
metres

CHAPEL

NAVE

CHANCEL

Monument at Middle Claydon   *Plan of Milton Keynes Church*

MONKS RISBOROUGH   St Dunstan

SP 813045

The angle-buttressed west tower and the nave and aisles are 14th century. The north transept walling may be 13th century but no early features survive. The south porch, the clerestory, and the chancel are 15th century, but externally were much restored in 1863-4. Also 15th century are three old bench ends and the screen. The four bay arcades have octagonal piers carrying arches with two sunk quadrants with broaches at their springing. The north transept has an image bracket and a canopied niche and there is another bracket by the pulpit. One window has fragments of old glass and there are a few old floor tiles. There are brasses of a civilian and wife of c1460, (half figures), and of the priest Robert Blundell, d1431.

MOULSOE   Assumption of the Virgin

SP 907418

Most of the church is 14th century, with window tracery with spheric triangles and quadrangles with trefoils and quatrefoils, and arcades of four bays of double-chamfered arches on octagonal piers. The tower top is later, and so are the plain square-headed clerestory windows without tracery. The chancel of 1773 was remodelled in 1861. There are a few old tiles in the south aisle. There are brasses to Richard Ruthall, d1528 and his wife.

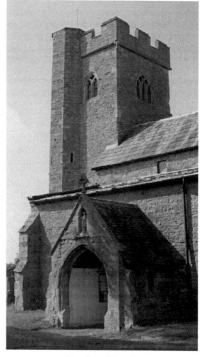

Moulsoe Church

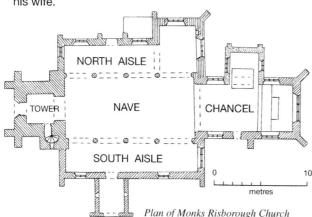

Plan of Monks Risborough Church

Monks Risborough Church

MURSLEY   *St Mary*   SP 817286

The nave and aisles with four bay arcades with octagonal piers carrying arches with one chamfer and one sunk quadrant and 14th century, but the buttresses, porch, clerestory and most of the windows date from a restoration in 1865-7. The 15th century west tower has a tower arch with three hollow chamfers. There is a Jacobean pulpit. A brass of Cecilia Fortescue, d1570 lies on a tomb chest. There is also an early 17th century monument to Sir Francis Fortescue and his wife, with kneeling mourners.

NEWPORT PAGNELL   *St Peter and St Paul*   SP 878440

The 14th century arcades of finely moulded arches on quatrefoil piers with shafts in the diagonals have five bays, then a length of wall before a 16th century sixth eastern bay which has replaced a central tower. The two storey north porch with a sexpartite vault, and the narrower south porch with blank arcading internally are also 14th century. The north aisle has 15th century windows, including one of five lights, but the south aisle was rebuilt in 1827-8. Also 15th century are the clerestory and the tie-beam roof with apostles, saints and angels on the wall-posts. The west tower with pairs of two-light bell-openings and clasping corner buttresses was added in 1542-8. The pinnacles on top are 19th century, when the chancel was much restored and large north vestries added. The only monuments of note are one with putti to Elizabeth Ann Revis, d1755, and a brass to a late 14th century civilian.

NEWTON BLOSSOMVILLE   *St Nicholas*   SP 926517

On the south side are sections of herringbone masonry, probably 11th century. There is also a 13th century lancet. The other features are mostly of c1300-40, with a pair of two bay arcades for the north aisle and north chapel, windows with flowing tracery in the chancel, a window with intersecting tracery in the nave, and one window with original stained glass in the aisle. The arcade west respond is a corbel with a head with arms. The chapel arcade has a quatrefoil-shaped pier. The 15th century west tower has a higher stair-turret and a sexpartite vault. The 15th century font has two-light blank panelling. The pulpit is of c1700.

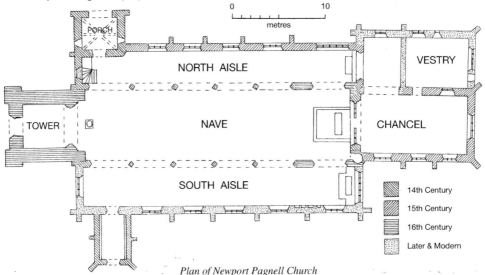

Plan of Newport Pagnell Church

Newport Pagnell Church   *Newport Pagnell Church*

NEWTON LONGVILLE   *St Faith*   SP 848314

The church looks all 15th century externally, with two porches, a west tower, roofs and many windows of that date. However the walls of both aisles and the chancel and north chapel are all 14th century, and the north doorway is 13th century. Inside are two bay arcades and chancel arch responds of c1185-1200. There are square abaci on the circular piers and responds. The south pier capital has upright leaves and the north one has a cat and a dog, whilst the chancel arch responds have crocket leaves and monsters. The arch itself was rebuilt later on from old parts. The font with patterns of lozenges and palmettes is Norman. It has a 17th century cover with alternating panels of lions and unicorns. The counterpoise is in the form of a dove with out-stretched wings. Only the head remains of a military effigy of c1300. There are a few old tiles.

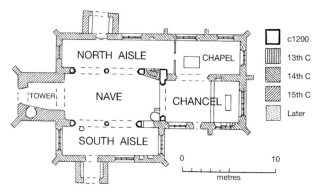

Plan of Newton Longville Church

Font at Newton Longville

NORTH CRAWLEY   *St Firmin*   SP 928447

North Crawley Church

The eastern corners remain of an early nave, although probably later than 1086, when a minster is recorded here in Domesday Book. Of c1200-10 is the five bay south arcade with double-chamfered arches on octagonal piers with leaf capitals. The western arches are lower and were clearly added after the original nave west wall was removed. The west tower with its circular SW stair-turret was added soon afterwards. The tower arch has three continuous chamfers. A now illegible inscription below the east window with its three foiled circles referred to St Firmin and Peter de Winton, rector here from 1294 until 1321. Other windows have bar-tracery and there is a double piscina. The top stage of the tower and the four bay north arcade with quatrefoil piers carrying double hollow-chamfered arches are 14th century. The aisles were rebuilt in the 15th century when the clerestory was added along with a tie-beam roof with figures of the Apostles standing above birds. There is a brass of John Garbrand, d1589 in the chancel. The octagonal font stands on trefoiled colonettes and has a cover dated 1640 with the initials T.L. and a castellated top. The 15th century screen has original painted figures of prophets and saints on the dado. There are straight-headed early 16th century bench ends with linenfold panelling, plus some benches in the south aisle dated 1635, again with the initials T.L, whilst the box pews of 1827 incorporate 17th century woodwork. There are Royal Arms of George III and a pulpit of the same period.

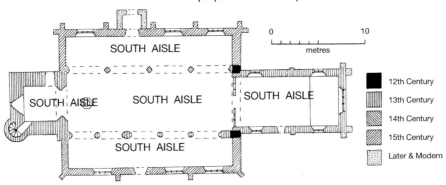

0   10

metres

SOUTH AISLE

SOUTH AISLE

SOUTH AISLE

SOUTH AISLE

SOUTH AISLE

■ 12th Century

▨ 13th Century

▨ 14th Century

▨ 15th Century

▦ Later & Modern

Plan of North Crawley Church

North Marston Church

NORTH MARSTON *St Mary* SP 777228

The north aisle with a west lancet is 13th century and has an arcade of double-chamfered arches on quatrefoil piers. The 14th century south arcade has two west arches with one sunk quadrant and one chamfer on piers which are concave-sided octagonal, plus an east bay with a moulded arch on piers with fleurons. More fleurons appear on the arch of the south aisle east window, which has image niches in the jambs. Bones found in a recess in the east wall in 1947 are thought to have been relics of John Shorne, rector here 1290-1314. He became famous for supposedly imprisoning the Devil in his boot and had a shrine here where a few old tiles remain. In 1478 it was transferred to St George's Chapel at Windsor Castle, the canons of whom probably built the chancel and embattled clerestory and nave roof with angels here to compensate the villagers for their loss of revenue from visitors. The chancel has fine sedilia with polygonally projecting canopies. Beside it is a two storey vestry with a stair-turret. The font has a renewed bowl resting on damaged angels. The stone book-rest in the south aisle has come from the church at Pitchcott. There are 15th century stalls with traceried fronts and misericords. There is a tablet to John Virgin, d1694.

OAKLEY *St Mary* SP 642122

The circular piers of the north arcade are of c1200, but the arches are 14th century, when the third arch was added to connect up with a newly begun west tower with cusped lancets and a tower arch of three continuous chamfers dying into the imposts. The south transept with reticulated tracery in the south window and an external cinquefoiled tomb recess below is mid 14th century. The transept east and west windows have original glass. The tower top with the stair-turret capped with a short stone spire is later, as are the windows of the chancel, the south aisle and the clerestory. There are two cross-slabs under plain recesses in the north aisle.

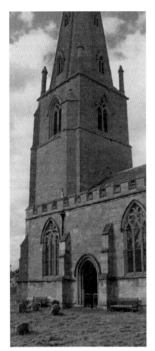

Olney Church

OLNEY   *St Peter and St Paul*   SP 890510

This is a large 14th century church with wide aisles with five bay arcades of arches with two sunk quadrants on quatrefoil piers and tall three-light windows with flowing tracery. In the chancel there is a tomb chest with quatrefoil panels forming an Easter Sepulchre on the north side (see picture on page 17), whilst the SW window has low-side openings under a transom. The east window dates only from 1874. The north aisle was partly rebuilt in 1807, when the porch was added and the clerestory removed. The south aisle windows were renewed in 1831. The tall west tower has a tall spire with ribs on the angles and four tiers of lucarnes facing the cardinal points. Pinnacles rise from low broaches at the corners. The pulpit is 18th century. The only monument of note is a modest tablet in the chancel to Catherine Johnson, d1680.

OVING   *All Saints*   SP 783214

Although much restored in 1867-9, the chancel is 13th century work with triple stepped east lancets and an inclination to the south. The arcades of double-chamfered arches on octagonal piers are late 13th century, although only one complete bay remains on the north side. A chapel with a reticulated east window was created on the south side in the 14th century. There is a large ogival-headed recess in the south wall. The clerestory and roof are 15th century (although the roof is dated 1657), and the west tower is early 16th century, but with a parapet of 1674. The screen and bench ends are late medieval.

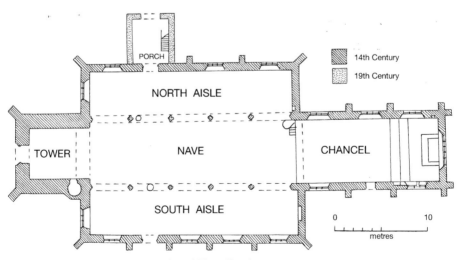

Plan of Olney Church

PADBURY *Nativity*

SP 722310

The chancel arch may be re-assembled work of c1200, the south aisle and its arcade is partly 13th century and the north arcade and tower arch are perhaps late 13th century, although the tower itself was rebuilt in 1800. The south doorway has nailhead decoration. The north aisle and chancel have 14th century windows and the circular windows of the north clerestory are of that date. The windows of the south aisle and south clerestory are 15th century. Only fragments remain of extensive wall-paintings.

Padbury Church

PENN *Holy Trinity* SP 917933

Over the north doorway is the date 1736 and the initials of Sir Nathaniel Curzon, who had the upper walls of the chancel and south chapel rebuilt in red brick, added the south porch and SW vestry, and carried the main roof down over the south aisle, the former clerestory being superseded by dormers in the roof. The west tower is 14th century and the north porch and the queenpost roof over the nave are 15th century. Arch braces on stone figures and heads help support the tie-beams. The south arcade is merely plain arches punched through an older wall, perhaps Norman. The Purbeck marble stem and base of the font are Norman. On boards over the chancel arch is a Doom painting of c1400, later simplified. There are brasses of three 16th century couples plus Elizabeth Rok, d1540 in her burial shroud, and others of William Penn, d1639, Lady Susan Drury, d1641, and John Penn, d1638. The many other monuments include that of Elizabeth Curzon, d1754, with a flat urn and a medallion portrait.

Penn Church

Monument at Quainton

PITCHCOTT   *St Giles*   SP 776204

This church was made redundant and is now occupied as a private house. The 13th century chancel retains one lancet. The nave may be older but has later medieval doorways and windows. The west tower is also late medieval. The south porch is dated 1662. The stone book-rest has been removed to North Marston.

PITSTONE   *St Mary*   SP 943147   ✓

This is another redundant church. It has a Norman font of the Aylesbury type with fluting on the stem and bowl and a recut top frieze. The narrow chancel and north chapel inclined to the north (see plan) are 13th century. What was once either a very wide nave or an unusually narrow nave with two aisles became a nave with a north aisle in the 15th century, with a new three bay arcade with double hollow-chamfered arches and new roofs. Also 15th century are the east end of the chancel and the north vestry. The west tower is if c1500. There are 16th century benches, 17th century box pews, 18th century altar rails and a Jacobean pulpit. The chancel has many medieval tiles. The Creed, Commandments and other texts with the date 1733 are painted over the chancel arch. The small brass found in 1935 may be of Lady Neyrut, c1325.

Preston Bissett Church

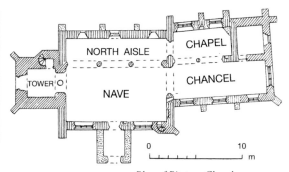

Plan of Pitstone Church

PRESTON BISSETT   *St John the Baptist*   SP 658291

The church is mostly 14th century and has three bay arcades of double-chamfered arches on octagonal piers, windows with flowing tracery (some with bits of old glass), a clerestory with three circular windows on each side, and a short west tower. Two crouching figures carry the chancel arch and the sedilia have head corbels carrying crocketed ogival arches. Outside the north aisle are reset Norman carved stones.

PRINCES RISBOROUGH   *St Mary*   SP 806035

Much was done to the church in 1867-8, when the vestry and organ chamber were added, and a new tower arch provided, although the tower itself is only of 1907-8. Some out of the seven narrow bays of arcade arches appear to be 13th century and there is a very fine shafted triplet of lancets of that period in the south aisle, which also has four ogival-arched 14th century tomb recesses and a fine sedile and piscina. There is a Jacobean pulpit with arabesque panels.

QUAINTON   *St Mary and Holy Cross*   SP 750201

The west tower and the nave and aisles with arcades of five bays are all 14th century, and the chancel is late 14th century, when it was widened northwards. Of the 15th century are the north chapel of two bays but with only a single arch with two hollow chamfers to the chancel, and the south aisle windows, one of which has an angle-piscina, an uncommon feature in Buckinghamshire, and the plain font. The arcades may also have been heightened. The north aisle windows appear to have been modified in the 17th century. However, the church was much restored in the 1870s. Part of the dado of the former chancel screen painted with the four prophets remains in the north aisle.

There are brasses to Joan Plessi, c1350, Margery Verney, d1509, a late 16th century lady and the priests John Lewys, d1422, and John Spence, d1485. There are kneeling effigies of Richard Brett, d1637 and his wife. He was one of the translators of the King James Bible. Under the tower is a monument to several 17th century members of the Dormer family. There are busts of Sir John Dormer, d1675 and his wife. A monument of 1689 has white figures of Richard Winwood with him recumbent and her half sitting up behind him. There are other monuments to Sir Richard and Thomas Pigott, c1736-40, Sir Robert Dormer, d1726 and his wife Mary and son Fleetwood.

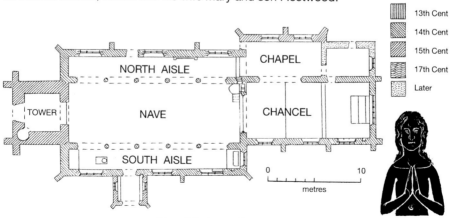

Plan of Quainton Church   *Brass at Quainton*

QUARRENDON   *St Peter*   SP 801159

By the site of the deserted village are featureless ruins of the nave west wall, the north aisle and the chancel. Nothing now remains of the former 13th century arcades.

RADCLIVE   *St John the Evangelist*   SP 676339

The south doorway of c1200-20 has two orders of shafts with shaft-rings, stiff-leaf capitals and a hoodmould of dogtooth over an arch with a roll-moulding within chevrons meeting at right-angles. Token beakheads on the chancel arch jambs may be of the same period, although the arch itself is later. The chancel is 13th century and has a 15th century east window in a surround made from older material. The west tower of c1300 has lancet windows and a doorway with continuous roll-mouldings. The nave has a big SE window of the 15th century and a timber-framed porch of c1500 in which are old benches with poppyheads. The tub font may be of c1200. There are Jacobean altar rails and fragments of 14th century stained glass in the nave north windows.

RADNAGE   *St Mary*   SU 787979

The nave, the central tower with its lancets, and the chancel with three separate east lancets are all early 13th century. Several windows are 14th century, including some reset when the nave was extended westwards and given a good tie-beam roof and a south porch in the 15th century. The upper parts of the chancel walls have been rebuilt in brick but the plain 16th century roof still remains. The font has a 17th century cover and there is a pulpit of c1700. Wall paintings range from patterns of c1200 over the tower west arch, 13th century figures around the east windows, part of a 15th century St Christopher on the nave north wall, and many good 16th to 18th century texts.

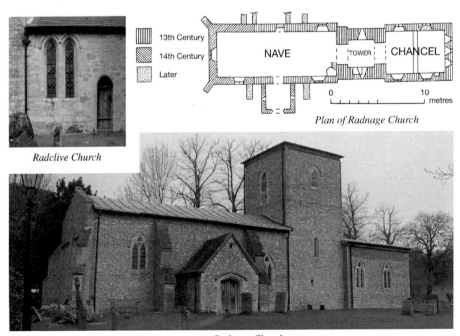

13th Century
14th Century
Later

NAVE   TOWER   CHANCEL

0   10
          metres

Plan of Radnage Church

Radclive Church

Radnage Church

Saunderton Church   Ravenstone Church

RAVENSTONE   *All Saints*   SP 851509

Parts of the nave and chancel north walls have herringbone masonry, probably of the 11th century. The two east bays of the south arcade are of c1190 with a circular pier with a waterleaf capital and a square abacus. The narrow arch into the 13th century west tower may be a later alteration. The chancel with one low-side lancet is also 13th century but its east wall seems to have been rebuilt. In the aisle are sedilia of c1300. The clerestory is 15th century. The south chapel was built to contain the large monument with a semi-reclining effigy of Heneage Finch, first Earl of Northampton, d1682. He had restored the church, providing the north buttress and south door dated 1670, in addition to the panelling, the pulpit with a large tester and some seats. The chapel has an original screen and altar rail with twisted balusters. The 13th century font has trefoiled arches and small quatrefoils, plus a 17th century cover.

ST LEONARDS   *St Leonard*   SP 910071

This is a single chamber with the walls battered internally. The roof with tie-beams and curved braces to the purlins is late 17th century when the church was restored from a ruinous state. The piscina and sedile are 14th century. The many 18th century monuments include a tablet of 1707 with two female mourners to Seth Wood and his wife, and a tablet and bust with putti on cannonballs to General Cornelius Wood, d1712.

SAUNDERTON   *St Mary*   SP 795019

The church was mostly rebuilt in 1888-91 but the windows and doorways are reused 14th century work and the shingled bell-turret with a steep pyramidal roof lies on medieval posts. The base remains of a timber chancel arch combined with the screen of c1400. There is a 13th century font of the Aylesbury type with a stiff-leaf foliage frieze. There are medieval tiles in the sanctuary.

SHABBINGTON   *St Mary Magdalene*   SP 666068

The eastern parts of the nave and the chancel north wall have herringbone masonry, probably of the 11th century. The church was much restored in 1877 and 1882 but has a 15th century nave roof with tie-beams and queen posts with what appears to be a canopy for a rood at the east end. Some 14th century windows escaped being renewed and there is an embattled west tower of c1500. The pulpit with foliage friezes is dated 1626. There are Royal Arms of George III on boards. By the porch is a 14th century cross-slab with an inscription in French.

SHALSTONE   *St Edward*   SP 641365

The chancel has some medieval walling and the north arcade piers may be late medieval, whilst the aisle itself was rebuilt in 1828. The rest was entirely rebuilt in 1861. There is a brass of Susan Kyngeston, and a monument of c1760 to Mrs Purefoy.

SHENLEY   *St Mary*   SP 832367

This is a cruciform Norman church and must always have had a central tower, although the existing tower, wider than the transepts and chancel, is 15th century work with three chamfers on the arches. Both transepts have Norman walling and a blocked east window remains in the south transept. Both aisles and the clerestory are 14th century and the four bay north arcade is of that date, but the south arcade of plain pointed arches set on short circular piers with moulded capitals and square abaci is of c1200. The chancel of the 1190s has a roll-moulding internally below the windows. A nailhead frieze goes over the windows, which have shafts with rings and crocket capitals. The keeled shafts on corbels flanked by other shafts higher up most have been intended for a vault. There are sedilia of the 13th century and a 15th century east window. The pulpit incorporates Jacobean panels. There are monuments to Sir Edmund Ashfyld, d1577, and Thomas Stafford, d1607, the last with a reclining effigy.

Shenley Church   *Chancel window at Shenley*

SHERINGTON *St Laud* SP 890469

The lower part of the central tower with tri-ple-shafted responds to the east and west arches is 13th century. The chancel is 14th century and so are the nave and aisles and the two storey south porch with a rib-vault. Just one window with flowing tracery appears to have survived the restoration of 1870. The arcades of four bays have bases so tall that the floor must have been low-ered. The north arcade is 13th century work. Of the 15th century are the large five-light west window, the clerestory, the south win-dows of the chancel, and the upper parts of the tower with unusual four-centred relieving arches high up on the exterior. The late 14th century font has figures of saints under flat ogival arches. The pulpit is early 18th cen-tury and the chandelier was given in 1783.

Interior of Sherington Church

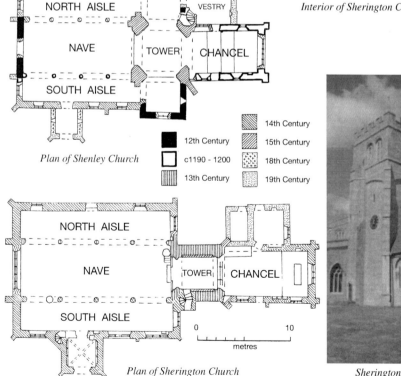

NORTH AISLE

VESTRY

NAVE TOWER CHANCEL

SOUTH AISLE

Plan of Shenley Church

	14th Century
■ 12th Century	15th Century
☐ c1190 - 1200	18th Century
▦ 13th Century	19th Century

NORTH AISLE

NAVE TOWER CHANCEL

SOUTH AISLE

0   10

metres

Plan of Sherington Church

Sherington Church

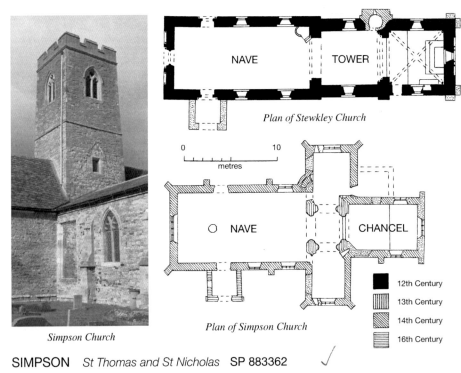

Plan of Stewkley Church

Plan of Simpson Church

Simpson Church

■	12th Century
▥	13th Century
▧	14th Century
☰	16th Century

SIMPSON   *St Thomas and St Nicholas*   SP 883362

The double-chamfered arches on semi-circular responds under the slender central tower are late 13th century. The chancel and wide nave and the transepts of differing sizes are all 14th century. Original are the nave doorways and windows and the ogival arched recess in the north transept, but the west window and the fine nave roof, plus the blocked squint towards the chancel from the south transept are 15th century, the south porch is 16th century and the transept roofs are 17th century. The chancel has been heavily restored, with its east wall rebuilt, and the former north vestry has gone.

SLAPTON   *Holy Cross*   SP 937208

The windows all look 15th century, but the arcades of double-chamfered arches on octagonal piers and the narrow aisles with their doorways are 14th century. The chancel was rebuilt with a brick outer facing in 1816, although it contains 14th century tiles. There are brasses of the priests Reynold Manser, d1642 and Thomas Knyghton, d1529, and of James Tournay, d1519 and his two wives. See photo on page 119.

STANTONBURY   *St Peter*   SP 836428

Only modest ruins remain of this church, which was left to decay in the early 20th century after its fine Norman chancel arch had been taken of to St James' at New Bradwell, a building otherwise of 1857-60. The arch has chevrons and beakheads and two orders of shafts with birds and beasts on the capitals. The nave was shortened by the building of the present west wall in the 15th century, and then in the 16th century it lost its north aisle but gained a porch in its place. There had also originally been a chapel on the south side of the chancel.

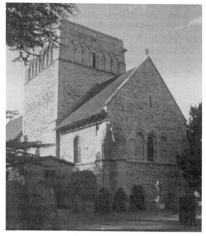

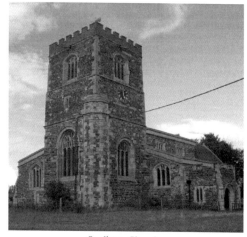

Stewkley Church   *Soulbury Church*

SOULBURY *All Saints* SP 882271

There are 14th century windows in the chancel and north aisle. The other windows, the clerestory and the west tower with a polygonal stair-turret all appear to be of c1480-1520. There are brasses of John Turnay, 1502 and his wife, and of the wife of John Mallet, d1516. Other monuments to the Lovetts of Liscombe Park include: Sir Robert, d1609 and wife both shown kneeling, Robert, d1699, Robert, d1740, Eleanor, d1786.

STEEPLE CLAYDON *St Michael* SP 705268

The chancel is 14th century and the wide nave has 15th century features. Brick transepts were added in 1842, and then a north aisle, vestry, porch and new chancel arch in 1858-9 whilst the steeple mentioned in the place name was added in 1862.

STEWKLEY *St Michael* SP 852261

This is the finest and least altered Norman church in Buckinghamshire, of c1150-80 and composed of a nave of three bays, a central tower and a square chancel beyond. Later features are confined to a low NE stair projection added to the tower in the 14th century, and a south porch and vestry added on the south side in the 19th century. The west front is similar to that at Iffley in Oxfordshire, having blank arches on either side of a doorway with scallops, foliage trails and beasts on the capitals. Two lunettes are cut out of the doorway tympanum, on which are dragons with twisted tails. There are chevrons on the arches. Above is a chevron course which goes round the entire church and then a window, plus another window in the gable, both adorned with chevrons. More chevrons appear on the east window and the blind arches flanking it, and on the north and south windows and the south doorway, which has one order of shafts and a hoodmould with pellets. The tower top has a blind arcade of intersecting arches. Yet more chevrons appear inside on a double frieze around all the windows, and on both the arches under the tower, which have scalloped capitals and an inner order of beak -heads, and also on the ribs of the vault over the chancel. The cells between the ribs now have brick infill of 1844 covered in paintings of the 1860s. There are two 15th century alabaster reliefs, one showing the Virgin and Child,. There are also a few old tiles.

STOKE GOLDINGTON   *St Peter*   SP 832472

The corners of the Norman nave remain, together with a plain chancel arch. The aisles with three bay arcades of double-chamfered arches on circular piers with circular abaci are 13th century, and the chancel and south chapel with windows with Y-tracery are of c1300. The west tower is 15th century and there is a plain clerestory of the 16th or 17th century on the south side. The early 18th century font has some marquetry.

STOKE HAMMOND   *St Luke*   SP 879299

This is a fairly small cruciform 14th century church. The tower arches only have responds to the east and west and seem to have been built in what was originally the east end of the nave. The chancel side windows have flowing tracery, but the east window, along with the ends of the transepts, the nave windows (one with old glass) and the south porch, are 15th century. The nave west end was rebuilt in 1852. The 14th century font has a quatrefoil bowl set on four shafts with their capitals penetrating into the re-entrant angles. The almsbox is dated 1618 on the supporting pillar. There is a monument of c1690 to various members of the Disney family.

STOKE MANDEVILLE   *St Mary*   SP 838095

The old church was blown up in 1966 and only minor ruins remain of it. A 15th century font, one old bench and the monument of c1600 to the Brudenell children now lie in the new church of 1866 1km to the NNW, where the modern village now lies.

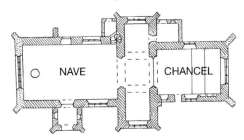

Plan of Stoke Hammond Church

Stoke Goldington Church

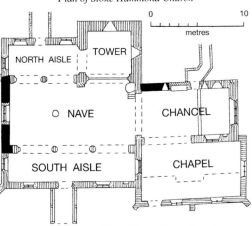

Plan of Stoke Poges Church

Stoke Poges Church

STOKENCHURCH   *St Peter and St Paul*   SP 834105

The round-headed SW window and the chancel arch with chevrons and keeled nook-shafts are of c1190. Just slightly later is the south doorway with an order of shafts and dogtooth on the hoodmould. The nave has a tall SE window of c1300-10 and there are others in the chancel, together with a good piscina. Also 14th century is the arch into a transept which was rebuilt in the 16th century. The arch became part of an arcade when a north aisle was added in 1893. There are brasses to two knights, d1410 and 1415, both called Robert Morle, and there are monuments to two men, d1680 and d1738, both called Bartholomew Tipping, plus a plain tablet to John Mason, d1765.

STOKE POGES   *St Giles*   SP 976828

The nave west wall and part of the chancel north wall with one window remain of the Norman church. The east end of the chancel and the north transeptal tower with lancets plus the south aisle with a three bay arcade are of the first half of the 13th century. The pyramidal roof of the tower was built in 1924 to replace a spire of 1702. The north aisle with a two bay arcade west of the tower is of later in the 13th century. Of the 14th century are the Easter Sepulchre tomb recess in the chancel north wall, the nave roof with tie-beams and kingposts with four-way struts and the fine timber-framed south porch with pairs of five ogival-headed side windows with quatrefoils in the spandrels.

From the chancel a wide arch opens into the brick Hastings Chapel of 1558 on the south side. The square-headed windows have remains of armorial glass. More old glass appears in the vestibule beyond the north doorway, including a hobby horse. The monuments in the chapel include a 13th century cross-slab with an inscription for William de Wytemerse, and a large cartouche with four cherubs probably for the Clarges family. Brasses of William Molyns, d1425 and his wife lie in the chancel. To the east of the churchyard lies a monument of 1799 commemorating Thomas Gray, and his Elegy in a Country Churchyard which had made Stoke Poges famous.

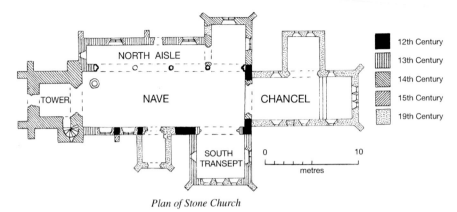

■	12th Century
▦	13th Century
▨	14th Century
▨	15th Century
▦	19th Century

Plan of Stone Church

STONE   *St John the Baptist*   SP 784122

Three bays of the north aisle and its arcade of round arches on circular piers with scallop and leaf-crocket capitals date from c1185-90. The west respond was moved further west and another pier inserted in the 13th century, when both nave and aisle were lengthened and the Norman south doorway with chevrons on the arch and an order of shafts was moved further west. A south transept was added, and then, c1275, a smaller north transept corresponding to one bay of the arcade. This transept has north window of two lights with a foiled circle. Only traces remain of a former clerestory and there is now a 19th century saddleback roof on the angle-buttressed 14th century west tower, whilst the 13th century chancel was mostly rebuilt in 1843 and 1900. From Hampstead Norris in Berkshire has come the Norman font with five panels of beaded interlace patterns with heads, beasts and symbols, although the iconographic significance of the scenes has been lost. There is also an 18th century font with four clustered piers, moved here a few years ago from the nearby St John's Hospital chapel, but originally in the church at Hartwell. There are brasses of William Gurney, d1472 and Thomas Gurney, d1520 and their wives.

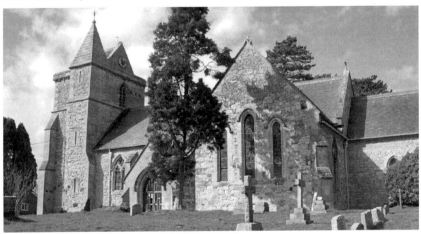

Stone Church

STONEY STRATFORD *St Mary & St Giles* ✓

SP 787404

Except for the 15th century west tower with clasping corner buttresses, the church was rebuilt after a fire of 1742 to a hall-church design with a nave and aisles of equal height by Francis Hiorn of Warwick. The clustered piers of wood, and the galleries on the north, west and south sides survived another fire in 1964. New tracery was put into the windows in 1876, a chancel was added in 1928, and new vestries in 1981.

STOWE *Assumption of the Virgin* SP 676574

The church lies alone within the park and is essentially 14th century except for the double-curved east gable of c1790 and the early 16th century north chapel with two bays of arches with panelling. The west tower has a niche with a miniature vault and buttressing over the west doorway. The east windows of the chancel and the south aisle both have reticulated tracery. Both arcades have three bays of double-chamfered arches on octagonal piers but that on the north may be late 13th century. The monuments include a much defaced 14th century effigy of a man in civilian dress, a small brass of Alice Saunders, d1462, and a white marble effigy showing Martha Penyston, d1619 in a burial shroud with a baby at her feet.

Stoney Stratford Church

SWANBOURNE *St Swithin* SP 801273 ✓

The 13th century chancel has three east lancets which internally form part of a five-arch arcade. The fine moulded south doorway is also 13th century work with seven cusps and one order of shafts. Of later in the 13th century are the tower arch and chancel arch with three hollow chamfers, the latter having corbels with trumpet scallops. The tower itself was rebuilt in the 15th century. There are several good late medieval style windows in the nave, although a datestone of 1630 records some rebuilding, and on the north side is a short aisle of c1500 with a rather crude arcade and a wall painting showing souls being taken either to heaven or hell. There is a brass to Thomas Adams and his wife. The inscription records he was "slain by bloudy theves" in Liscombe Park in 1626.

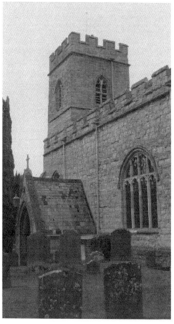

Swanbourne Church

TAPLOW   *St Nicholas*   SP 912822

The church of 1828 was enlarged in 1865 and mostly rebuilt in 1911-12. From the old church which lay further west near the manor house have come the Norman font of Purbeck marble with blank arches on each side, and brasses of Richard Manfeld, d1455 with his brother and sister and that Nichole de Aumberdene, a small figure of c1350 in civilian dress set in the head of a foliated cross.

TATTENHOE   *St Giles*   SP 830339

The 13th century base of the 17th century font is the only relic of the original church. The existing single chamber within the suburbs of Milton Keynes is said to have been built c1540 using materials from Snelsall Priory and has windows with square labels. The box pews, pulpit, altar rails and flooring are all of c1800.

THORNBOROUGH   *St Mary*   SP 744337

The herringbone masonry on the south side of the nave probably dates from the 11th century. The north arcade is 13th century and c1300 the chancel was lengthened and given an east window with intersecting tracery. The low-side NW window looks slightly later. The three circular clerestory windows on the north side and the windows with flowing tracery in the north aisle are 14th century. The west tower and the windows with panel tracery, plus the tiles in the aisle and nave are and some old glass in the chancel SW window are 15th century. There are brasses of William Barton, d1389 and his wife, and there is also a tablet to Charles Wodnoth, d1778.

Plan of Tattenhoe Church

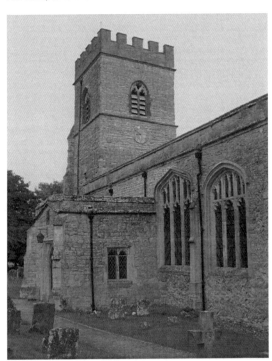

Thornborough Church

Tingewick Church

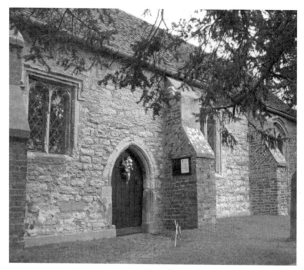

Tattenhoe Church

Tingewick Church

THORNTON   *St Michael*   SP 753363

The nave with a trail frieze on the outside, the aisles, chancel arch and west tower are all 14th century. The box pews, two-decker pulpit, squire's pew and west gallery are all late 18th century, and it was probably then that the clerestory windows were blocked up and the chancel demolished. There are mid 15th century alabaster effigies of John and Isobel Barton, and good brasses under a canopy set on a tomb chest of Robert Ingylton, d1472 and his three wives.

TINGEWICK   *St Mary Magdalene*   SP 659331

There are chevrons on the round arches of the Norman north arcade. The western pier is a chamfered square instead of circular and the last arch is pointed and narrower, suggesting that c1200 both nave and aisle were lengthened by a bay. The chancel and the slim west tower are 15th century. The south aisle was added in 1852. In the aisle is the mechanism of an early 17th century turret clock. A brass of Erasmus Williams, d1608 shows him facing the pillar of the Temple (the church) and away from the arts.

TURVILLE   *St Mary*   SP 767911

A plain Norman doorway remains on the north side, and the south doorway, chancel arch and tower arch all look 13th century. The priest's doorway and an adjacent window in the chancel are 14th century. Of the 16th century are the west tower with a later brick parapet, the crown-post roof with four-way struts, the benches at the west end and remains of a screen under the tower. The brick north aisle with two transverse gables and an arcade of plain round arches dates from 1733 and contains a monument of 1740 to members of the Perry family, The porch was also added about then. There is some heraldic glass of the 16th and 18th century and the altar rails are Jacobean.

TURWESTON   *Assumption of the Virgin*   SP 601378

The external details are of 1863, when the west tower was rebuilt with a saddleback roof and the vestry and south chapel added. Both aisles are mostly 14th century, when they were widened, and one arcade arch on the south side is of that date, but the north aisle was originally of c1190 and the south aisle of c1210, Each retains a west window and a two bay arcade of their respective dates. In each case the arcade pier is more in the nature of responds on either side of a short section of wall, with waterleaf, crockets and stiff-leaf on the northern capitals. The chancel arch and chancel are also early 13th century, with lancets on each side but a 15th century east window and an ogival arched 14th century recess on the north side. The nave roof has 16th century tie-beams. There are brasses to a mid 15th century priest and Thomas Grene and two wives of c1490, plus a tablet to Symon Haynes, d1628.

TWYFORD   *Assumption of the Virgin*   SP 665266

The north aisle is very narrow and the south aisle is three times its width and looks as if it was widened in the 15th century to match the extent of a former south chapel or transept which once had a large triple east lancet. This means the splendid Norman south doorway may have been reset twice. There are beasts on the capitals of the three orders of shafts, beakheads on the arch and a tier of stars on each jamb. Parts of the chancel arch with chevrons and beakheads are Norman too. Both arcades are of four bays with quatrefoil piers and are 13th century, the southern side being the earlier. Each side has a later fifth bay embracing the west tower of 1300 with a later top stage. The chancel has 13th century walling, but its features are all later, such as the 14th century sedilia and the plan 16th century roof. The nave roof with tie-beams on arch braces, kingposts and diagonal struts is slightly earlier, and the aisle roofs are partly old too. The porch is most probably 15th century and the dates 1619 and 1833 refer to repairs. There are a complete set of old benches with trefoiled poppyheads, the dado of a screen and a Jacobean pulpit.

Of the late 13th century is a Purbeck marble effigy of a cross-legged knight with his hand on his breast. There is a crude bust holding a heart under an ogival-headed tomb recess in the south aisle. There are brasses of the priest John Everden, d1413, and Thomas Gyffard, d1550, the latter set on a tomb chest and having earlier engravings on the reverse. A monument with a cartouche of Richard, first Viscount Wenman, d1640 lies between two other monuments, one of which is to Richard Wenman, d1572. The churchyard cross base with trefoiled arches round the corners is 13th century.

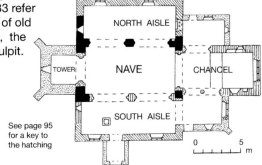

See page 95 for a key to the hatching

Plan of Turweston Church

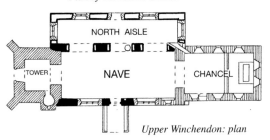

Upper Winchendon: plan

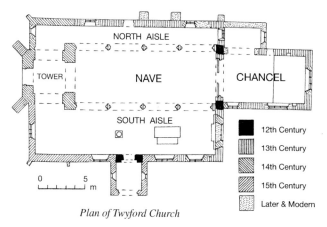

Plan of Twyford Church

NORTH AISLE

TOWER   NAVE   CHANCEL

SOUTH AISLE

0   5   m

■ 12th Century

▨ 13th Century

▧ 14th Century

▨ 15th Century

▨ Later & Modern

TYRINGHAM

St Peter   SP 860467

Only the west tower and a brass of Mary Catesby, d1508, survived the total rebuilding of the church in 1871 as a memorial to the wife of W.B.Tyringham. The tower has a 16th century belfry stage set on a Norman lower stage with a single-stepped tower arch.

UPPER WINCHENDON   *St Mary Magdalene*   SP 745145

The aisle added in the late 12th century to the nave has an arcade of three plain round arches cut through the older wall. Of the same period is the fine south doorway with one shaft twisted and the other adorned with lozenges. There are scallopoed capitals and the arch has a roll-moulding. In the nave SE corner is a Norman window set in a recess with a low sill forming a seat. The early 13th century chancel has three lancets on each side and two facing east. The windows with flowing tracery in the north aisle are 14th century, and two south windows and the diagonally buttressed west tower with a spirelet on the stair-turret are 15th century. The wooden pulpit with a crenellated top is 14th century and there is an old screen plus some early 16th century benches. There is a brass to the vicar Sir John Studeley, d1502. See photo on page 119.

Norman doorway at Upper Winchendon

Tyringham Church

South arcade at Waddeston Church

Norman doorway at Upton

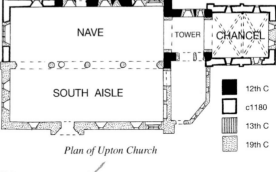

NAVE | TOWER | CHANCEL

SOUTH AISLE

■ 12th C
□ c1180
▨ 13th C
▦ 19th C

Plan of Upton Church

UPTON   *St Laurence*   SU 981791

The central tower and the eastern two thirds of the nave with a blocked window and a restored doorway with one order of shafts are Norman work of c1150-60. The west end of the nave and the rib vaulted chancel are addition of c1180. The vault ribs have rolls on an unmoulded band and rest on corbels, whilst a plain arch set on semi-circular shafts divides the two bays, the capitals all having scallops. The set of three arches at the east end of the wide south aisle added in 1850 originally lay at the east end of the nave. One arch is 12th century and the other two are 13th century, one of which (now in the middle) is of oak and has bands of dogtooth and shafts with crocket capitals. The font is also Norman and has tall blank arches on thin colonettes. In the tower south wall is a 15th century alabaster of the Trinity. There are brasses of a knight and two wives of c1520 and of Edward Bulstrode, d1599 and his wife.

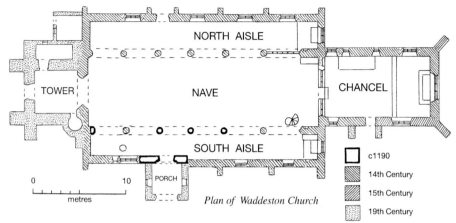

NORTH AISLE

TOWER

NAVE

CHANCEL

SOUTH AISLE

PORCH

0   10

metres

Plan of Waddeston Church

- ☐ c1190
- ▨ 14th Century
- ▨ 15th Century
- ▨ 19th Century

WADDESTON   *St Michael*   SP 740170

Of c1190 are the south doorway with a pointed arch with chevrons at right angles and trumpet scallops on the shafts and the central bays of the south arcade with scallop capitals on the piers, which also have brackets for intended tranverse arches or wooden wall-posts. The west respond was moved one bay westwards when the nave and aisle were lengthened both to the west and east in the early 14th century. Two more east arches with complex mouldings were then created and a north aisle with a six bay arcade and windows with Y-tracery was added. The tower arch and the chancel are also 14th century, although the tower itself was entirely rebuilt in 1891, whilst the chancel gained some new windows and buttresses in the 15th century, when the nave clerestory was added. The octagonal font with quatrefoil panels is also 15th century. The seat with a canopy in the south aisle is probably French work of the early 16th century. The once fine (but now fragmentary) brass of Roger Dynham, d1490 under a canopy was brought here from a chantry chapel at Eythrope in 1892. There are also brasses of the priest Richard Huntyngdon, d1543, Hugh Brystowe, d1548 in his burial shroud, and Robert Pygott, d1567 and his wife, on the reverse of which are earlier engravings of a figure in a shroud and a lady.

Waddeston Church

Walton Church   *Westbury Church*

WALTON   *St Michael*   SP 885369

The church now serves the Open University, which is based in this part of Milton Key-nes. The whole building appears to be 14th century, although the west tower and south porch appear to be later than the nave and chancel. The tie-beam roof of the nave has a medieval form but details suggesting it is of c1600. There are good busts in oval medallions of Bartholomew Beale, d1660 and his wife. A monument of c1780 by Nollekens has a bust of Sir Thomas Pinfold, d1701.

WATER STRATFORD   *St Giles*   SP 652343

The 14th century west tower has lost its original top. The nave and chancel were rebuilt in 1828 but the Norman doorways and windows of the 14th, 15th and 17th centuries were re-used. The south doorway has an order of shafts with interlace on the capitals and an arch of chevrons over a tympanum showing Christ in Majesty supported by two angels, under which is a frieze of tiny intersecting arches. The other doorway, now on the north side of the chancel, has the Lamb and Cross set against a diaper background on a tympanum over a lintel with two Viking-style intertwined dragons.

WAVENDON   *St Mary*   SP 911372

The exterior details are all of the remodelling of 1848, but two windows have 14th cen-tury glass, the tower is 15th century, and the arcades and chancel arch are late 13th century with arches with one chamfer and two hollows over quatrefoil piers. There is a good tablet to George Wells, d1713. From St Dunstan-in-the-West, London, has come the fine late 17th century pulpit with cherub heads and pendants of flowers and fruit.

WENDOVER   *St Mary*   SP 871074

The tower arch, chancel arch and the arcades are all 14th century. The arches have sunk quadrant mouldings and the western piers are octagonal. The square eastern piers with semicircular shafts with beasts and heads amongst the foliage capital are late 14th century. In the south aisle is a tablet to William Edmunds, d1768. The exterior is almost all of the restorations of 1838-9, 1868-9 and 1914. Two older windows are reset and there is a 14th century doorway with ballflowers in the former south porch.

Norman doorway at Water Stratford

WESTBURY *St Augustine* SP 622356

The saddleback roof on the 13th century west tower and the north porch, the buttresses and windows date from 1863. Inside are three bays of double-chamfered 14th century arches on octagonal piers. Medieval tiles remain in the chancel and some old glass is reset in the vestry.

WESTON TURVILLE *St Mary* SP 859103

The chancel arch (later widened) and three bays of the south aisle with a doorway and an arcade of double-chamfered arches with original wall paintings set on slim circular piers are 13th century. The 14th century chancel has a good double piscina but the east window is of 1860. However, this window and several others do contain fragments of old glass. The nave was lengthened in the 14th century and given a new five bay arcade on the north side and two extra bays on the south. In the 15th century a west tower was set mostly within the west bay of the nave and the north aisle and chapel built, the roofs also being of that period. There is a Norman font of the Aylesbury type with a band of leaf scrolls over fluting and a reversed block capital with decorated lunettes forming the base. Part of a 14th century screen remains in the south aisle, and there is a mid 17th century pulpit. There is a brass of a civilian of c1580.

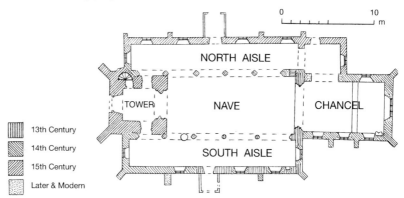

Plan of Weston Turville Church

WESTON UNDERWOOD   *St Laurence*   SP 864504

The SE corner of a Norman nave still remains. Aisles were added in the 13th century but the eastern piers of the arcades seem to have been given new bases and abaci in the 14th century, which is the period of the doorways and chancel arch. Following a rise in status in 1376 from chapel-of-ease to Olney up to being a parish church the building was remodelled with a full set of new windows including a large east one with a transom and surviving original glass. The west tower was then added and a new font was provided, on which are the arms of John Olney, d1405. Of his brass only the surrounding inscription recording the church's rise in status still remains. There is a brass to Elizabeth Throckmorton, d1571, and also another monument of c1690 to several members of the Throckmorton family. The pulpit and the altar rails are also of that period, whilst the box pews are late 18th century.

WEST WYCOMBE   *St Laurence*   SU 87828950

The church lies high above the present village and seems to have originally served the vanished village of Haveringdon. The long 13th century chancel retains traces of its priest's doorway and former windows and the east window cuts into a small circular upper window. In c1750-2 Sir Francis Dashwood had the 14th century west tower heightened and furnished with a golden ball with seating for ten people which also acted as an eyecatcher from the main house and his house, where the members of his Hellfire Club held twice yearly orgies. In c1755-60 Sir Francis built a large new nave in the form of "a very superb Egyptian Hall", with giant attached columns around the walls, actually of brick but plastered and painted to imitate porphyry. There is a rich entablature frieze, and a flat painted ceiling. The chancel was also remodelled and given a fine painted ceiling with a barbed quatrefoil containing a copy of Rubens' Last Supper. The reredos, altar rail, stalls, and panelling are all contemporary. The font stand has a claw tripod with a serpent winding up a shaft and about to devour a dove, whilst four other doves are grouped around where the tiny bowl would be. The monuments include one to Sir Francis' father and namesake, d1724, and another of c1710-15 to Hugh Darrell, d1667, with his wife and grandson.

West Wycombe Church

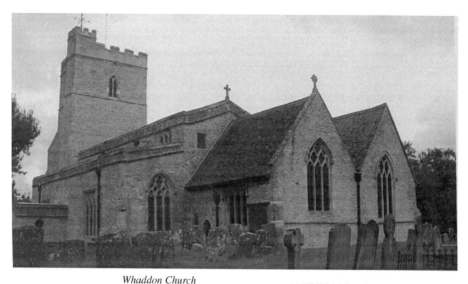

Whaddon Church

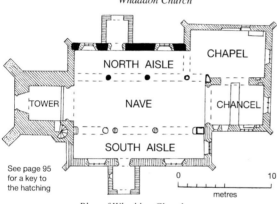

Plan of Whaddon Church

See page 95 for a key to the hatching

WHADDON   *St Mary*   SP 805341

WEXHAM   *St Mary*
SU 993815

Both the chancel and nave are Norman, with one original north window and a circular west window in the latter. Quoined projections of on each side (now lost on the south) towards the west end hint at a possible huge former tower as at Fingest. If the early 14th century are the east window with cusped intersected tracery and an ogival-headed crocketed recess in the chancel south wall.

Most of the church is 14th century, with plain sedilia of that period in the chancel, some original glass in the south aisle east window, and a diagonally buttressed west tower. The arcades have arches of that date but the piers and the aisle walls are older, of c1175 on the north side, where one pier has two peacocks fighting over food, and of c1200-10 on the south, where there are leaf capitals except one older one with scallops. The narrower east bay on the north is of the latter period and now opens into a large north chapel, the north wall of which was rebuilt in 1889. The north and south porches both appear to be 16th century. The 13th century font lies on four shafts separated by vertical bands of dogtooth. The animal-face bracket on the adjacent pier would have carried a pulley to raise the former cover. The altar rail is Jacobean. On the back plate of a monument in the chapel that probably served as an Easter Sepulchre are brasses of Thomas Pygott, d1519, and two wives. There is also a tomb chest of Lord Grey de Wilton, d1593 and his wife.

WHITCHURCH   *St John the Evangelist*   SP 803209

The church of the 1290s has side windows of two lights with bar tracery in the form of a sexfoiled circle and an east window of three lights with a circle enclosing a concave-sided lozenge. Both the priest's doorway on the south and the doorway to a former north vestry have continuous sunk-quadrant mouldings. A broad segmental arch covers a stepped seat of sedilia and there is a double piscina. The south arcade with circular piers may also be 13th century and with it would go a reset lancet in the aisle west wall. Both arcades have double-chamfered arches, that on the north being 14th century with octagonal piers and thus of the same period as both the aisles and the angle-buttressed west tower mostly set within the nave, with the aisles extending for a fifth bay to flank it. The arches under the tower are triple-chamfered. The doorway with three orders of shafts with stiff-leaf capitals is reset 13th century work. On the tower south face is a big sundial dated 1628. The clerestory and roof are 15th century, and so probably is the south porch, the date 1657 on it referring only to a repair. The south aisle has a roof dated 1681, and the brick buttress is probably also of that date. The font has a stone bowl dated 1661 on a wooden column. There are stall ends with tracery and poppyheads with the initials of Robert Hobbs, last Abbot of Woburn, c1529-38, and there are also benches with poppyheads. There are fragments of 14th century glass in the chancel windows, and 15th century wall paintings showing St Margaret with a dragon in the south aisle. The poorbox and pulpit are Jacobean. There is a monument to Ann Gaderen, d1599 in the chancel.

WILLEN   *St Mary Magdalene*   SP 879412

This brick church with stone dressings replaced a decayed Norman building and was built in 1679-80 to a design by Robert Hooke for Dr Richard Busby, headmaster of Westminster School. It has a tower flanked by small chambers used as a vestry and library, a nave with the round arched window heads penetrating into an imitation barrel-vault, and a lower apse of 1861 replacing the original square chancel. The doorway into the porch under the tower lies within a deep recess. The tower orginally had a domical cap of lead. The original furnishings include pews, the hexagonal pulpit, and a white marble font with cherubs' heads on a black polygonal baluster and with a ogival-shaped cover with flowers, fruit, angels, cherubs and an urn on top.

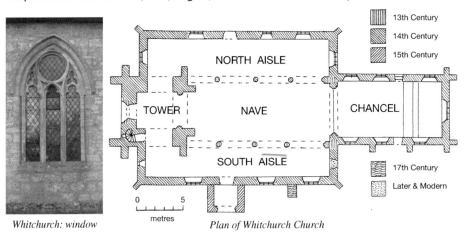

▨	13th Century
▨	14th Century
▨	15th Century
≈	17th Century
▦	Later & Modern

NORTH AISLE

TOWER   NAVE   CHANCEL

SOUTH AISLE

0   5
metres

Whitchurch: window   *Plan of Whitchurch Church*

Willen Church

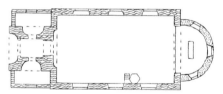

Plan of Willen Church

The north arcade at Whitchurch

Sedilia and piscina at Whitchurch

Font at Whitchurch

WING   *All Saints*   SP 880226

This is one of England's most important Saxon churches, probably begun in the early 9th century. It consisted of quite a long nave flanked by aisles, with four bay arcades of plain round arches punched through the nave walls. The doorways high up at the west end of the nave suggest there must have been a timber gallery. A crypt to the east of the nave was begun at the same time it, and later divided into an octagonal inner area presumably for relics, and a surrounding ambulatory for pilgrims reached by a staircase from a doorway in the north aisle. Finally a polygonal apse with angle pilasters carrying a blind arcade was raised over the crypt. Over the chancel arch (which has probably been widened) is an original Saxon two-light window with the arches formed of tiles and a baluster shaft between them. No other original windows survive.

The eastern arches of the arcades were made wider in the late 13th century. The south aisle was rebuilt in the 14th century when the north aisle was given new windows. The south porch, clerestory and the west tower with set-back angle buttresses were added in the 15th century, which is also the date of the rood screen. The north vestry and the three lunette windows lighting the crypt are 19th century.

In the porch is the reversed two-scallop capital type base of a Norman font of the Aylesbury type with foliage in the lunettes. There is also a loose Norman capital. In the nave is a 15th century font with half figures of angels and shields with the Instruments of the Passion. There are traces of 13th century wall paintings on the north arcade. The south aisle east window has fragments of old glass. There is a fine monument of c1575 for Sir Robert Dormer. There are recumbent effigies of Sir William Dormer, d1575, and his wife, and kneeling effigies of the first Lord Dormer, d1616 and his wife, and a bust of Lady Anne Sophia Dormer, d1695. Other monuments include brasses of Harry Blaknall, d1460 and a civilian of c1470 and their wives, a brass to Thomas Cotes, d1648, a slab to Bridgett Neale, d1677, and a putto and urn to Henry Fynes, d1758.

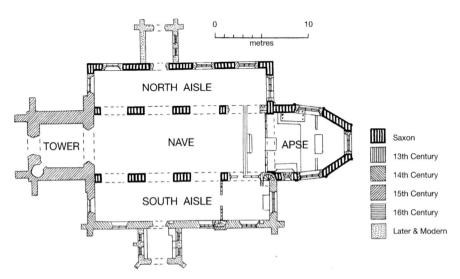

Saxon	
13th Century	
14th Century	
15th Century	
16th Century	
Later & Modern	

Plan of Wing Church

Wing Church

Interior of Wing Church

Wingrave Church

WINGRAVE

St Peter & St Paul   SP 880226

The north wall of the chancel of c1190 has internal blind arcading on short shafts with leaf capitals. The fourth arch is lower than the other three. Similar arcading on the south side is more fragmentary. Beyond the north wall is a narrow chamber with a pointed tunnel vault and 13th century wall paintings that might have once been an anchorite's cell. The external doorway to it is modern. One original lancet remains in the chancel, which also has a cusped lowside lancet of c1300.

The tower arch is triple chamfered with stiff-leaf capitals typical of the 13th century and has a 15th century screen, but the tower itself was mostly rebuilt in 1898. The five bay arcades of double-chamfered arches on octagonal piers are 14th century. Most of the 15th century windows were renewed in the restoration of 1887-9. There is a rope band carved on the Norman font. Twelve 15th century male figures form wall-posts for the nave roof and there are angels with shields on the end of the principals of the north aisle roof.

WINSLOW   *St Laurence*   SP 768275

The lower part of the west tower engaged by the aisles and the four bay arcades of double-chamfered arches on octagonal piers, the foiled circular clerestory windows and the chancel are all 14th century. The five-light east window of the chancel, several other windows, the south porch and the tower top are 15th century. The half-timbered east gable of the chancel probably dates from the restoration of 1883-4, and the north chapel is of 1889. There is a good Jacobean font with a book-rest and the nave has a fine 18th century chandelier. In north aisle are faded wall paintings of c1500 showing a Doom scene with the Virgin in Glory (i.e. as a judge) next to Christ, St Christopher with an inscription including the word "safe" and the Martyrdom of St Thomas Becket.

Interior of Wingrave Church

WOLVERTON   *Holy Trinity*   SP 804413

This church lies in the village of Old Wolverton, now part of Milton Keynes. It is mostly a neo-Norman structure of 1809-14 but is said to incorporate an old tower. Inside is a semi-reclining effigy of Sir Thomas Longville, d1685 dressed in Roman armour.

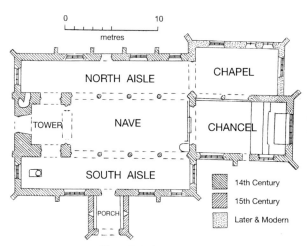

0   10
metres

NORTH AISLE

CHAPEL

TOWER   NAVE

CHANCEL

SOUTH AISLE

PORCH

▨ 14th Century

▧ 15th Century

▨ Later & Modern

Plan of Winslow Church

Winslow Church

Norman chancel arch at Worminghall

WOOBURN   *St Paul*   SU 909879

The 12th century arcades were rebuilt in 1856-7 and in 1868-9 the nave and chancel were embattled, the windows given new tracery, and the 15th century west tower was given a parapet and cap to the stair-turret. There are brasses of John Godwyn d1488 and his wife Pernell "first founders of the stepull", Christopher Askowe and his wife c1510, the priest Thomas Swayne, d1519, and a man of c1520 in a burial shroud. Other monuments are Arthur, infant son of Philip, Lord Wharton, d1641, and Philip, 4th Lord Wharton, d1695.

WORMINGHALL   *St Peter and St Paul*   SP 642080

Norman are the chancel arch with an order of shafts with volute capitals rising from chevrons and the south doorway with an order of shafts with capitals with leaves ending in corbels. The north doorway was renewed in 1847 when the whole of that side of the nave was rebuilt as part of a restoration costing £1200. The south side was also much repaired and given a new porch and a vestry. The brass of Philip Kinge, d1597 and his wife shows a chrysom child at their feet.

Worminghall Church

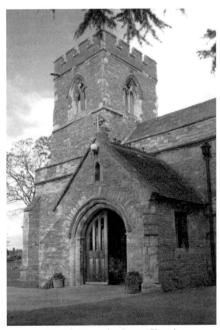

Woughton on the Green Church

WOTTON UNDERWOOD *All Saints*   SP 688159

The 14th century chancel and the nave with its 15th century features but possibly older walling were much restored in the mid 19th century, along with the chantry chapel of 1343 on the south side which had previously been rebuilt in 1710. Part of a Norman frieze of saltire crosses remains over the doorway between the tower and the nave. Monuments include two kneeling figures and a recumbent female effigy of the late 16th century and brasses of Edward Grenville, d1585 and his wife on a slab with an incised marginal inscription.

WOUGHTON ON THE GREEN *Assumption of the Virgin*   TQ 001740

This church lies within Milton Keynes. The west tower may be 15th century but the nave and south aisle with an arcade of double-chamfered arches on quatrefoil piers, plus the south porch and the chancel are all 14th century. The chancel has a south window with reticulated tracery and an ogival-headed tomb recess in which is a defaced effigy of a priest. The window tracery is mostly of the restoration of 1865-7, when the vestry was added. There is a good tablet to Martha James, d1775.

WRAYSBURY *St Andrew*   SP 879412

The chancel arch and arcades of c1200 have square piers with nook-shafts which continue to form keeled roll-mouldings on the otherwise plain pointed arches. In 1862 the north aisle was mostly rebuilt and the lost former south aisle replaced, whilst the west tower with its broach-spire is of the 1870s. However one blocked original lancet remains in the chancel where original wall paintings also survive. There is a pulpit of c1700. There are brasses of a knight and lady of c1500 under a double canopy and of John Stonor, d1512 in an academical gown. Other monuments include that of Harriett Paxton, d1794.

FURTHER READING

The main sources are Elizabeth Williamson's revised 1994 edition of the 1960 Buckinghamshire volume by Nikolaus Pevsner in the Buildings of England series, the two volume Buckinghamshire gazetteer of ancient monuments published by the Royal Commission on Ancient and Historical Monuments in 1912, and several Buckinghamshire volumes of the Victoria County Histories. See also: Murray's Buckinghamshire Architectural Guide of 1948 by John Betjeman and John Piper; Monumental Brasses, The Portfolio Plates of the Monumental Brass Society, of 1988.

Slapton Church

Upper Winchendon Church

A GLOSSARY OF TERMS

Abacus	-	Flat slab on top of a capital on a column, pier or respond
Apse	-	Semicircular or polygonal east end of a church containing an altar
Ashlar	-	Stone blocks with even faces and square edges set close together.
Ballflowers	-	Globular flower of three petals enclosing a ball. Common c1310-40.
Baroque	-	A whimsical and odd form of the Classical architectural style.
Broaches	-	Sloping half-pyramids adapting an octagonal spire to a square tower.
Cartouche	-	A tablet with an ornate frame usually enclosing an inscription.
Ceilure	-	An ornate part of a wagon roof above the rood-loft or altar.
Chancel	-	The eastern part of a church used by the clergy and choir.
Chevrons	-	Vs usually arranged in a continuous sequence to form a zig-zag.
Clerestory	-	An upper storey pierced by windows lighting the floor below.
Coffered	-	Decorated with sunk square or polygonal panels.
Crossing Tower	-	A tower built upon four arches in the middle of a cruciform church.
Cruciform Church	-	Cross shaped church with transepts forming arms of the cross.
Cusp	-	A projecting point between the foils of a foiled Gothic arch.
Dado	-	A decorative (usually blank arcaded) lower part of a wall or screen.
Dogtooth	-	Four-cornered stars placed diagonally and raised pyramidally.
Easter Sepulchre	-	A recess in a chancel which received an effigy of Christ at Easter.
Fleuron	-	Decorative carved flower usually with four petals.
Foil	-	A lobe formed by the cusping of a circle or arch.
Head Stops	-	Heads of humans or beasts forming the ends of a hoodmould.
Hammerbeam Roof	-	Roof carried on arched braces set on beams projecting from a wall.
Herringbone Masonry	-	Courses of stones alternately sloping at 45 degrees to horizontal.
Hoodmoulding	-	A narrow band of stone projecting out over a window or doorway.
Impost	-	A wall bracket, often moulded, to support one end of an arch.
Jamb	-	The side of a doorway, window or other opening.
Lancet	-	A long and comparatively narrow window. Usually pointed headed.
Lintel	-	A horizontal stone or beam spanning an opening.
Low-side Window	-	A window with a low sill allowing anyone outside to see an altar.
Lucarnes	-	Small openings for light set on the sides of a stone spire.
Misericord	-	Bracket below a hinged choir stall seat to support a standing person.
Mullion	-	A vertical member dividing the lights of a window.
Norman	-	A division of English Romanesque architecture from 1066 to c1200.
Nave	-	The part of a church in which the congregation stood or sat.
Ogee-headed window	-	Topped by a curve which is partly convex and partly concave.
Pediment	-	Low pitched gable over portico, doorway, window or end of building.
Piscina	-	A stone basin used for rinsing out holy vessels after mass.
Purlin	-	Horizontal beam intermediate between the wall-plate and ridge beam
Putti	-	Small naked cherubs or boys forming parts of funerary monuments.
Quoin	-	Dressed stone at the corner of a building.
Rere-arch	-	An arch on the inside face of a window embrasure or doorway.
Reredos	-	A screen or structure behind or partly above an altar.
Respond	-	A half-pier or column bonded into a wall and carrying an arch.
Reticulation	-	Tracery with a net-like appearance.
Rood Screen	-	Screen with a crucifix mounted upon it between a nave and chancel.
Sedilia	-	Seats for clergy (usually three) in the south wall of a chancel.
Spandrel	-	The surface between two arches or between an arch and a corner.
Tie-Beam	-	Horizontal transverse beam spanning a room at wall-plate level.
Tierceron	-	Secondary rib between a main springer or central boss to another rib.
Trefoiled	-	Composed of three segments of circles.
Tympanum	-	The space between the lintel of a doorway and an arch above it.
Wall-Plate	-	A beam set on top of a wall to carry the ends of the rafters.